英语知识点强化练习(下)

主　编　崇永民　邢月娥　许婷婷
副主编　董慧欣　阮洁云

北京理工大学出版社
BEIJING INSTITUTE OF TECHNOLOGY PRESS

版权专有　侵权必究

图书在版编目(CIP)数据

英语知识点强化练习. 下 / 崇永民, 邢月娥, 许婷婷主编. --北京：北京理工大学出版社, 2023.5
　ISBN 978-7-5763-2419-8

Ⅰ. ①英… Ⅱ. ①崇… ②邢… ③许… Ⅲ. ①英语课-中等专业学校-升学参考资料 Ⅳ. ①G634.413

中国国家版本馆 CIP 数据核字(2023)第 097052 号

出版发行 / 北京理工大学出版社有限责任公司
社　　址 / 北京市海淀区中关村南大街 5 号
邮　　编 / 100081
电　　话 / (010)68914775(总编室)
　　　　　(010)82562903(教材售后服务热线)
　　　　　(010)68944723(其他图书服务热线)
网　　址 / http://www.bitpress.com.cn
经　　销 / 全国各地新华书店
印　　刷 / 定州市新华印刷有限公司
开　　本 / 787 毫米×1092 毫米　1/16
印　　张 / 11　　　　　　　　　　　　　　　责任编辑 / 王晓莉
字　　数 / 225 千字　　　　　　　　　　　　　文案编辑 / 王晓莉
版　　次 / 2023 年 5 月第 1 版　2023 年 5 月第 1 次印刷　　责任校对 / 周瑞红
定　　价 / 35.00 元　　　　　　　　　　　　　责任印制 / 边心超

图书出现印装质量问题，请拨打售后服务热线，本社负责调换

前　言

本书依据《中等职业学校英语课程标准（2020年版）》，结合中等职业学校就业与升学的实际情况而编写。

本书能够夯实学生的英语学习基础，适用于所有中职学生的英语学习。共分为8个单元，每个单元所附的习题，以 Warming up、Listening and Speaking、Reading and Writing、Grammar 以及 More Activities 5 个模块的形式展开，呈现方式多样化，以语音、填空、选择、对话练习、完形填空、阅读理解、改错及写作的练习方式帮助学生掌握词汇、课文内容和语法知识，使其拓展知识面，提高英语水平。针对学生高考的需求，在每个单元的学习内容结束后，本书又附有单元检测习题，习题内容符合对口英语高考大纲，且题型与高考题型一致，能有效地达到举一反三、灵活运用所学知识点的目的，可以帮助学生在日常学习中巩固基础、提高技能。本书很好地满足了职业学校的学生参加职教高考的需求。

我们本着"注重基础，突出运用，精选内容，强化训练，提高分数"的原则，力争做到"由浅入深、循序渐进"，符合中等职业学校学生的认知特点和接受能力。本书可作为中等职业学校教师的复习教学用书，也可作为一、二年级学生日常学习用书，而对于参加对口升学的毕业班学生来说，其同样适用。

本书的作者均是来自教学一线、有多年教学经验的教师。但由于水平有限，疏漏与不足之处在所难免，恳请各位老师、同学及其他读者批评指正。

编　者

目 录

Unit 1　A Small Change Can Solve the Problems of Many ················ 1
 Warming up ·· 1
 Listening and Speaking ·· 2
 Reading and Writing ·· 4
 Grammar ·· 6
 More Activities ·· 9
 单元检测 ·· 10

Unit 2　It's Always Nice to Be Polite ·· 19
 Warming up ·· 19
 Listening and Speaking ·· 20
 Reading and Writing ·· 21
 Grammar ·· 24
 More Activities ·· 26
 单元检测 ·· 28

Unit 3　We Are Part of Nature ·· 37
 Warming up ·· 37
 Listening and Speaking ·· 38
 Reading and Writing ·· 40
 Grammar ·· 43
 More Activities ·· 46
 单元检测 ·· 47

Unit 4　Beauty Is About How You Feel ·· 56
 Warming up ·· 56
 Listening and Speaking ·· 57
 Reading and Writing ·· 58
 Grammar ·· 61

More Activities	64
单元检测	65

Unit 5 It's Necessary to Develop Soft Skills ... 74

Warming up	74
Listening and Speaking	75
Reading and Writing	77
Grammar	80
More Activities	83
单元检测	84

Unit 6 It's like a Home Away from Home ... 93

Warming up	93
Listening and Speaking	95
Reading and Writing	96
Grammar	99
More Activities	101
单元检测	103

Unit 7 High Technology Has Really Changed Our Life ... 111

Warming up	111
Listening and Speaking	112
Reading and Writing	113
Grammar	116
More Activities	119
单元检测	120

Unit 8 I Have a Dream ... 129

Warming up	129
Listening and Speaking	130
Reading and Writing	132
Grammar	135
More Activities	137
单元检测	138

Unit 1

A Small Change Can Solve the Problems of Many

Warming up

一、句型总结

1. It's the third time I've lost a transit card. 这是我第三次丢交通卡了。

2. So we wouldn't need to reach for it every time we use it. 这样我们就不必每次用到时伸手去拿了。

3. Brilliant! You're more creative than I am. 太棒了！你比我更有创意。

4. How can I join your club? 我怎么样才能加入你们的俱乐部？

5. The club was set up by a group of like-minded students. 俱乐部是由一组趣味相投的学生创建的。

6. It means that you will have a good chance to broaden your mind. Sounds fun. 这意味着你们有很好的机会开阔心胸，听起来很有趣。

7. Just fill out an application form. It's all free. 只要填写一张申请表就可以了。它是完全免费的。

8. We live in an age of innovation, when creativity is of increasing value. 我们生活在一个

创新的时代,创造力越来越有价值。

9. Creativity is important not only for artists and writers but also for those who work in the professions such as scientists and engineers. 创造力不但对艺术家和作家重要,对那些诸如科学家和工程师等从事专门职业的人来说也重要。

10. For those who want to make their mark, continuous innovation can be the key to success. 对于那些想有所成就的人来说,不断创新会是他们成功的关键。

11. We may think a creative person just comes up with new ideas by accident, but actually that's not the case. 我们可能认为一个有创造力的人只是偶然有了新想法,但事实上不是那样的。

12. We are all influenced by things around us and things we have been exposed to, but creative people pay more attention to their surroundings. 我们都被周围的事物影响,但有创造力的人更关注他们周围的事物。

13. He made his mark as a pianist in the 1920s. 在20世纪20年代他作为一名钢琴家很成功。

14. If it is a legal matter, you need to seek professional advice. 如果是法律的事情,你需要寻求专业的建议。

二、英汉互译

1. 有创造力的_____   2. 垃圾桶_____
3. 数据线_____   4. 好奇的_____
5. 解决_____   6. 意见;看法_____
7. 设计_____   8. 组织;安排_____
9. 增长;扩大_____   10. 申请表_____

Listening and Speaking

一、找出与所给单词画线部分读音相同的选项

(　　) 1. d<u>u</u>stbin   A. c<u>u</u>rious   B. l<u>u</u>xury   C. v<u>a</u>lue   D. infl<u>u</u>ence
(　　) 2. s<u>o</u>lve   A. d<u>o</u>nate   B. pr<u>o</u>fession C. ec<u>o</u>nomic D. c<u>o</u>nflict
(　　) 3. <u>un</u>likely A. <u>o</u>pinion   B. d<u>e</u>sign   C. br<u>i</u>lliant D. <u>in</u>ventive
(　　) 4. v<u>a</u>lue   A. <u>o</u>rganize   B. w<u>a</u>terproof C. d<u>a</u>ta   D. im<u>a</u>ginative
(　　) 5. n<u>ea</u>t   A. l<u>ea</u>k   B. l<u>ea</u>ther C. sw<u>ea</u>ter   D. br<u>ea</u>k

Unit 1 A Small Change Can Solve the Problems of Many

二、从B栏中找出与A栏中相对应的答语

A

1. How do you like it?
2. What kind of activities do you do?
3. Have you got any better ideas?
4. What a bad day today! Why?
5. How can you become creative?

B

A. Well, we do a lot of things, like designing cultural signs and slogans.
B. I can use my imagination.
C. I enjoy it very much.
D. I think the card could be made like a bracelet.
E. I lost my transit card.

1. _____ 2. _____ 3. _____ 4. _____ 5. _____

三、补全对话

A: Good morning, Janet. __1__ Where did you buy it?

B: Thank you. I made it by myself.

A: __2__

B: I changed my jeans into this bag, and the four pockets are useful.

A: __3__ You are so smart.

B: I like DIY and always make something from second-hand items. You can try, __4__

A: Thank you for your suggestion. I have a lot of second-hand things. __5__

> A. How did you make it?
> B. Your bag looks cool.
> C. Wow, it's such a creative idea.
> D. I believe I can change them into new ones.
> E. and you will discover the joy of DIY.

四、情景模拟(主题对话)

编写一组对话,写明如何加入俱乐部。

set up / join your club / activities / broaden your mind / fill out an application form / have a good chance to

_____

_____

_____

Reading and Writing

一、用所给词的适当形式填空

1. Having a _____ (creativity) mind allows us to do new and exciting things.

2. With your _____ (permit), I would like to visit the institute.

3. The public opinions are _____ (influence) by the media nowadays.

4. If you hear the _____ (continue) fire alarm, you must leave the building by the nearest exit.

5. Human beings are different from animals, because they can _____ (inventive) more and more tools and machines.

6. It is a _____ (垃圾桶) that helps sort rubbish.

7. A small change can _____ (解决) the problems of many.

8. What kind of _____ (活动) do you do?

9. It means that you will have a good chance to _____ (拓展) your mind.

10. Teaching is his _____ (职业).

二、完形填空

Using computers is part of our life. On the Internet, we can read news, plan holidays, pay bills, make __1__, play games and so on. But for some people, once they are onto the Internet, they just can't stop.

It __2__ that 51% of the men and 42% of the women think Internet is one reason why they're not getting enough __3__! 68% of the Internet addicts say they have less time to stay with their family or to visit their friends face to face than before.

Some students also have Internet addiction. These students often stay __4__ school and home and throw their homework away, just playing games in the Internet cafes. They __5__ the screens straight, and their fingers hit keys quickly. At times, they shout loudly and jump from their seats when they win or lose the games. These "gamers" play games most of the day, then think about

Unit 1　A Small Change Can Solve the Problems of Many

them for　6　of the day and dream about them in bed at night. They soon become lonely and won't talk with others. They think about nothing　7　the results of the games they have got. They prefer playing computer games to　8　. Computers are now their　9　friends.

That makes their parents　10　.

Unless we can use computers in a right way, our life will be worse and worse.

(　) 1. A. friend   B. mistakes   C. friends   D. friends with
(　) 2. A. was reported   B. is reported   C. reports   D. reporting
(　) 3. A. sleep   B. sleeping   C. sleeps   D. slept
(　) 4. A. away   B. far   C. away from   D. from
(　) 5. A. watch   B. walk   C. look   D. hear
(　) 6. A. others   B. another   C. the rest   D. other
(　) 7. A. except   B. besides   C. beside   D. near
(　) 8. A. study   B. studying   C. studies   D. studied
(　) 9. A. best   B. the best   C. well   D. better
(　) 10. A. to worry   B. worrying   C. worried   D. worries

三、阅读理解

阅读下面短文,从每题所给的 A、B、C、D 四个选项中选出最佳答案。

Paper is one of the most important products ever invented by man. The invention of paper means that more people could be educated because more books could be printed. Paper provides an important way to communicate with knowledge.

Paper was first made in China about 2,000 years ago. In Egypt and the West, paper was not very commonly used before the year 1400. Paper was not made in southern Europe until about the year 1100. After that, the forestry countries of Canada, Sweden, Norway, Finland, and the United States became the most important paper-making countries. Today Finland makes the best paper in the world. And it has the biggest paper industry in the world.

When we think of paper, we think of newspapers, books, letters, envelopes, and writing paper. So paper plays an important role in our lives.

Paper is very good for keeping you warm. Houses are often insulated with paper. You perhaps have seen homeless men sleep on a large number of newspapers. They are insulating themselves from the cold. In Finland, in winter it is sometimes 40 degrees below zero. The farmers wear paper boots in the snow. <u>Nothing could be warmer.</u>

(　) 1. What does the invention of paper mean?
　　A. It means more people could be educated.

B. It means more books could be printed.

C. It means paper is one of the most important products.

D. It means paper is invented by man.

(　　)2. When was paper made in southern Europe?

  A. Before 1100. B. After 1400. C. After 1100. D. Before 1400.

(　　)3. Which country makes the best paper?

  A. Norway.   B. Canada.

  C. The United States.   D. Finland.

(　　)4. What's the meaning of the underlined sentence "Nothing could be warmer"?

  A. Books are warmer.   B. Newspapers are warmer.

  C. Paper is the warmest.   D. Houses are the warmest.

(　　)5. What's the main idea of the passage?

  A. The invention of paper.   B. The best paper.

  C. The paper-making.   D. The uses of paper.

四、书面表达

以"My opinion on creativity"为题,写一篇文章,字数80~100字。

_____

_____

_____

_____

_____

_____

Grammar

一、从下面每小题四个选项中选出最佳选项

(　　)1. —Could you do me a favour?

  —It depends on _____ it is.

  A. which B. what C. that D. how

(　　)2. It's foggy outside. I can't understand _____ Mr. Brown insisted on driving to the downtown.

Unit 1　A Small Change Can Solve the Problems of Many

  A. why B. whether C. how D. what

(　　)3. I don't know _____ or not they will come to help us.

  A. that B. if C. whether D. how

(　　)4. —What are you talking about?

  —We are talking about _____.

  A. how can we get there B. we can how to get there

  C. how we can get there D. what can I do to get there

(　　)5. We have known _____.

  A. that smoking can do harm to our health

  B. whether can smoking do harm to our health

  C. why can smoking do harm to our health

  D. how smoking can do harm to our health

(　　)6. This computer looks great. I wonder _____.

  A. how much does it cost B. how much it costs

  C. how much cost it is D. what it cost

(　　)7. I wondered what _____ him so excited.

  A. make B. makes C. made D. to make

(　　)8. He told me that the film _____ for ten minutes.

  A. had been on B. had begun C. has been on D. is to be

(　　)9. I knew that the sun _____ in the east when I was very young.

  A. will rise B. rose C. rises D. to rise

(　　)10. I don't think he is fit for the job, _____ he?

  A. isn't B. is C. was D. am

(　　)11. He wanted to know _____ the English party.

  A. when will we have B. when we will have

  C. when would we have D. when we should have

(　　)12. Do you know _____?

  A. which is this used for B. what this is used for

  C. which this is used D. that this is used for

(　　)13. He told me that he _____ a cold for three days.

  A. has B. had caught C. had had D. has had

(　　)14. It hasn't been decided yet _____ this weekend.

  A. where will they have dinner B. where they will have dinner

  C. where having dinner D. where did they have dinner

(　　)15. Mr. Zhang is to give us a report on _____ in Korea.
　　　　A. what he sees and hears　　　B. what does he see and hear
　　　　C. what he saw and heard　　　 D. what did he see and hear

(　　)16. I don't know _____ to go.
　　　　A. if　　　B. /　　　C. whether　　　D. it

(　　)17. I don't remember when we _____.
　　　　A. arrive　　　B. would arrive　　　C. arrived　　　D. arriving

(　　)18. Do you know _____ time the plane leaves ?
　　　　A. when　　　B. what　　　C. if　　　D. where

(　　)19. He asks whether his father _____ back tomorrow.
　　　　A. will come　　　B. comes　　　C. came　　　D. would come

(　　)20. The teacher said that the sun _____ around the earth.
　　　　A. travelled　　　B. travel　　　C. travels　　　D. travelling

(　　)21. He said that they _____ members of the Party since 1948.
　　　　A. were　　　B. are　　　C. had been　　　D. have been

(　　)22. I don't know what _____ to buy.
　　　　A. does he want　B. he wants　　　C. did he want　　　D. he wanted

(　　)23. Would you like to know when he _____ back.
　　　　A. would come　B. comes　　　C. will come　　　D. came

(　　)24. We're worried about _____ he is safe.
　　　　A. if　　　B. whether　　　C. that　　　D. /

(　　)25. I'm sure _____ our team will win.
　　　　A. that　　　B. /　　　C. whether　　　D. A and B

(　　)26. He asks _____ I like playing the piano.
　　　　A. that　　　B. whether　　　C. what　　　D. /

(　　)27. Could you tell me how _____ the station.
　　　　A. can I get to　B. do I get to　　　C. I got to　　　D. to get to

(　　)28. He insists that he _____ with us.
　　　　A. should go　　B. went　　　C. goes　　　D. will go

(　　)29. He wondered if _____ the meeting the next week.
　　　　A. they will have　　　B. will they have
　　　　C. they would have　　　D. would they have

(　　)30. The expressions they use depend on _____ they speak to.
　　　　A. that　　　B. who　　　C. whom　　　D. /

二、找出下列句子中错误的选项，并改正过来

1. I wonder that June is a good time to visit Hong Kong.
       A   B C   D

2. I don't know if he will come home for the festival or not.
              A   B   C   D

3. We are talking about if we'll go on the picnic.
        A   B   C   D

4. The teacher told us the earth turned around the sun.
              A   B   C   D

5. Could you please tell me where is the supermarket?
   A   B   C   D

6. I didn't remember where have I seen the man before.
   A   B   C   D

7. Bill asked whether Job has given the note to their father.
        A   B   C   D

8. We are talking about if he can be admitted into our club.
        A   B   C   D

9. I don't know what to solve the problem.
             A   B   C   D

10. You should understand who are you at first.
              A   B   C   D

More Activities

一、找出与所给单词画线部分读音相同的选项

( ) 1. und<u>er</u>line   A. pion<u>ee</u>r   B. waterp<u>r</u>oof   C. ins<u>er</u>t   D. <u>e</u>mergency

( ) 2. de<u>s</u>ign   A. tran<u>s</u>it   B. <u>s</u>eal   C. <u>s</u>witch   D. in<u>s</u>titute

( ) 3. swit<u>ch</u>   A. stret<u>ch</u>   B. stoma<u>ch</u>   C. <u>ch</u>ef   D. <u>Ch</u>ristmas

( ) 4. <u>e</u>conomic   A. mor<u>e</u>over   B. conv<u>e</u>nience   C. conflict   D. b<u>e</u>come

( ) 5. <u>u</u>nlikely   A. val<u>u</u>e   B. <u>u</u>seful   C. <u>u</u>mbrella   D. tr<u>u</u>th

二、汉译英

1. 越来越有价值_____   2. 想出；提出_____

3. 不仅……而且……_____   4. 偶然_____

5. 比如；例如_____   6. 不是那样的_____

7. 成功；成名_____   8. 使……接触到_____

9. 天生；天性_____   10. 编造_____

三、用所给单词的适当形式填空

1. _____(creative) is very important in doing new things.

2. The idea of _____(make) glasses came from Nero who watched his fights using a transparent green stone.

3. We are easily _____(influence) by the media nowadays.

4. You will see to be _____(continue) at the end of this book.

5. As we all know, _____(inventive) plays an important role in our life.

6. Do you know who _____(invent) the first light blub.

7. _____(tradition) fans with blades are often unsafe.

8. Whether _____(permit), I would like to visit the institute.

9. If it is a legal matter, you need to seek _____(profession) advice.

10. There are many creative _____(activity), and I've made several interesting friends there.

四、找出下列句子中错误的选项,并改正过来

1. Moreover, although they have switches, we often forget switching them off.
      A   B   C   D

2. In addition, the socket can operated through a free app.
     A   B   C   D

3. The blades are hid inside the base of the fan.
      A   B   C   D

4. Thank to the egg carton, it's convenient for people to store and transport eggs.
      A   B   C   D

5. I didn't know who invents the waterproof camera.
     A   B C   D

单元检测

第一部分 英语知识运用(共分三节,满分40分)

第一节 语音知识:从 A、B、C、D 四个选项中找出其画线部分与所给单词画线部分读音相同的选项。(共5分,每小题1分)

( )1. creativity   A. century   B. calculator   C. celebrate   D. cycle

Unit 1 A Small Change Can Solve the Problems of Many

(　　)2. data　　　A. cable　　　B. brilliant　　　C. application　　　D. access

(　　)3. influence　　A. curious　　B. value　　C. put　　D. luxury

(　　)4. theme　　A. therefore　　B. thirty　　C. breathy　　D. thus

(　　)5. leak　　A. break　　B. breakfast　　C. headache　　D. neat

第二节　词汇与语法知识：从 A、B、C、D 四个选项中选出可以填入空白处的最佳选项。(共 25 分，每小题 1 分)

(　　)6. Today, people are living in _____ of information and technology explosion.
　　A. a year　　B. an age　　C. a date　　D. a day

(　　)7. The artist is not only gifted _____ hard-working.
　　A. but also　　B. also　　C. and　　D. too

(　　)8. _____ thinkers can change the world.
　　A. Creativity　　B. Creative　　C. Create　　D. Creation

(　　)9. Most people think that confidence is the key _____ success.
　　A. in　　B. of　　C. to　　D. for

(　　)10. If he can _____ more attention to his health, he won't stay in hospital now.
　　A. pay　　B. have　　C. play　　D. get

(　　)11. There are several ways to solve this problem. _____, asking for help from your colleagues.
　　A. Because　　B. For example　　C. As if　　D. Such as

(　　)12. The study shows how people _____ by TV advertisements.
　　A. are made　　B. are sold　　C. are influenced　　D. are told

(　　)13. Ancient people tried all _____ of plants and found some of them were edible.
　　A. ways　　B. sorts　　C. pairs　　D. toys

(　　)14. Little children may feel uneasy in the unfamiliar _____.
　　A. surroundings　　B. work　　C. weather　　D. way

(　　)15. The new-media industry favors young people _____ are creative.
　　A. which　　B. whose　　C. who　　D. why

(　　)16. Imagination is of great _____ to every child, and it is the same with adults.
　　A. value　　B. valuable　　C. valueless　　D. valued

(　　)17. The elderly are confused when they _____ a lot of information on the Internet.
　　A. are exposed to　　B. meet with　　C. are missing　　D. are met

(　　)18. After winning the prize, the young writer _____ overnight.
　　A. made marks　　B. made his mark　　C. made a mark　　D. marked

(　　) 19. Eddie loves her job as a doctor and she works her way to the top of her _____.

  A. life   B. job   C. profession   D. work

(　　) 20. Travelling is good for our body because the long walks provide a lot of exercise. _____, it is good for our mind because it relieves stress and anxiety.

  A. However   B. In addition   C. Above all   D. Finally

(　　) 21. We won the game _____ a lot of hard work and the cooperation between the team members.

  A. thanks to   B. despite   C. as a result   D. although

(　　) 22. It is necessary _____ us _____ do sports every day.

  A. of; to   B. for; to   C. of; by   D. to; for

(　　) 23. The bad weather conditions prevented our plane from landing. _____, the plane was able to land safely at last.

  A. Fortunate   B. Unfortunately   C. Fortunately   D. Unfortunate

(　　) 24. Wi-Fi _____ by Vic Hayes in 1977, who has been called the "father of Wi-Fi".

  A. is invented   B. was invented   C. invented   D. inventing

(　　) 25. _____ her illness, she carried on working as usual.

  A. But   B. In spite   C. Despite   D. For

(　　) 26. I don't know _____ the girl is talking about.

  A. that   B. what   C. why   D. whether

(　　) 27. The screen of the mobile phone is large so that it is easy for elderly _____.

  A. to be operated   B. operating   C. to operate   D. operated

(　　) 28. I would like to rent a house, modern, comfortable, _____ in a quiet neighbourhood.

  A. above all   B. in all   C. after all   D. at last

(　　) 29. Please don't forget _____ the windows if you leave the house.

  A. close   B. closed   C. closing   D. to close

(　　) 30. —Excuse me, could you tell me _____?

  —Certainly.

  A. when can I get to the station   B. I can get to which station

  C. which station can I get to   D. how I can get to the station

第三节　完形填空：阅读下面的短文，从所给的 A、B、C、D 四个选项中选出最佳的答案。(共10分，每小题1分)

  In the Eastern Han Dynasty (25-200)(东汉), a court official named Cai Lun __31__ a new kind of paper from bark (树皮), fishnet, wheat stalks (秆) and other __32__. It was relatively cheap, light, thin, durable and more suitable for brush writing.

The __33__ of paper-making spread east to Korea and Japan at the beginning of the seventh century. In the eighth century, along with the Silk Road, the Arab countries began to learn __34__ to make paper. It took about 400 years for paper __35__ traverse(穿过) the Arab world to Europe. In the 14th century many paper factories __36__ in Italy, from which the workmanship of paper-making spread to the European countries such as Germany. The Italians produced the material in a __37__ number and exported(出口) large amounts of it, dominating (主导) the European market for many years. In the 16th century, the art of paper-making appeared in Russia and Holland, __38__ it spread to Britain in the 17th century. With the invention of paper, the popularization of knowledge has __39__ into reality. The invention of paper is an epoch-making(划时代的) event in __40__ history.

( )31. A. made   B. held   C. built   D. borrowed
( )32. A. rooms   B. ways   C. challenge   D. materials
( )33. A. part   B. art   C. letter   D. influence
( )34. A. why   B. what   C. how   D. where
( )35. A. in   B. to   C. for   D. from
( )36. A. were set up B. was cut off C. were sold   D. was sent
( )37. A. small   B. little   C. many   D. large
( )38. A. although   B. if   C. and   D. but
( )39. A. gong   B. turned   C. called   D. returned
( )40. A. human   B. earth   C. health   D. animal

第二部分 篇章与词汇理解(共分三节,满分50分)

第一节 阅读理解:阅读下列短文,从每题所给的A、B、C、D四个选项中选出最恰当的答案。(共30分,每小题2分)

A

Perhaps you have heard a lot about the Internet, but what is it?

The Internet is many different networks around the world. A network is a group of computers that are put together. These networks joined together are called the Internet.

Maybe that doesn't sound interesting. But when we've joined the Internet, there are lots of things we can do. We can have a lot of fun on the World Wide Web(www). We can use the Internet instead of a library to find all kinds of information for our homework. We can find information about our favorite sports or film stars and do shopping on the Internet. We can also send messages to other people by e-mail. It is much cheaper and quicker than calling our friends or sending a letter.

With the help of the Internet, the world is becoming smaller and smaller. People can now work at home with a computer in front of them, getting and sending the information.

They can buy or see the things that they want on the Internet. But do you know 98% of the information is in English? So what will English be like tomorrow?

( )41. The passage is mainly about _____.

  A. the Internet B. information C. computers D. email

( )42. The quickest and cheapest way for people to send messages to their friends is _____.

  A. by post B. by e-mail C. by telephone D. by TV

( )43. The Internet cannot be used to _____ according to the passage.

  A. find information for our homework

  B. get some information about our favorite sports stars

  C. do some shopping

  D. do our housework

( )44. Which of the following is NOT true?

  A. The Internet is a big computer.

  B. The Internet is lots of computer networks.

  C. The Internet is very helpful.

  D. People can work at home with the help of the Internet.

( )45. What does the writer try to tell us with the last two sentences?

  A. The Internet is more and more popular.

  B. All the information is in English.

  C. English is important in using the Internet.

  D. Every computer must join the Internet.

B

A great new invention by a British student will help children who are overweight. It will also reduce the number of hours of television they watch every day. The technology is nicknamed "Square-Eyes". It is a tiny, computerised sensor (感应器) that fits into children's shoes. It measures the number of steps the child takes during the day and sends the information to the family computer. Software then tells the child how many hours of TV he or she can watch that evening. One hundred steps equal one minute of TV. If children use up all of their viewing time, they must do more walking.

The designer Gillian Swan says this will help children to include exercise in their daily life

Unit 1 A Small Change Can Solve the Problems of Many

from an early age. Ten years ago, children were healthier because they played outside with their friends. But today's children spend too much time in front of TV and don't exercise. This means children have weight problems and become fat. "Square-Eyes" is a nickname often given to children who watch too much television. It may now have a new meaning. The new technology is the beginning of computers that become a part of our clothes. What we wear will soon <u>monitor</u> our health.

(　　) 46. "Square-Eyes" can help children who have _____ problems.
　　　A. eyesight　　　B. weight　　　C. feet　　　D. walking

(　　) 47. Where can we find "Square-Eyes" on children?
　　　A. In children's pockets.　　　B. In children's head.
　　　C. In children's shoes.　　　D. In children's schoolbags.

(　　) 48. If Jimmy wants to watch TV for twenty minutes, he should walk _____ steps.
　　　A. twenty　　　B. two hundred
　　　C. two thousand　　　D. twenty thousand

(　　) 49. What does the underlined word "monitor" mean in Chinese?
　　　A. 执行　　　B. 促进　　　C. 影响　　　D. 监控

(　　) 50. What's the purpose of this invention?
　　　A. To help children take more exercise.
　　　B. To prevent children from getting up late in the morning.
　　　C. To encourage children to play outside with their friends.
　　　D. To help children sleep well.

C

Have you noticed your life becoming a little easier? Now, when you go to a certain shopping mall, you can enjoy its free Wi-Fi there. When you want to take a taxi, you can book one with your smart(智能的) cellphone. In fact, all these can be seen as the basic parts of a smart city.

The idea of a smart city was brought up by US Company IBM in 2010. Generally, a smart city is a city that uses modern technologies such as the Internet to improve city planning, save money and resources, and make our life <u>convenient</u>. How smart can a city become? Here are great examples.

In 2009, Dubuque became the first smart city in the US. The city used smart water meters(水表) to take the place of traditional water meters. They can detect(探测) water waste and leakage (泄漏) and send data to let the house owner know. The same system is used for other city resources like electricity and natural gas. By this way, people know how much they have used and are glad to help reduce waste.

　　Santander in Spain also gives us a look at the future. If people point a cellphone toward a nearby bus stop, the phone can show all the bus lines that serve the stop. The government has also organized a research team and provided an app(应用程序) that collects data on almost everything: light, temperature, and the movements of cars and people. Opening the app near a supermarket, it can provide the immediate information on special offers.

(　　)51. What makes the life easier than it used to be?
　　　　A. Free Wi-Fi.　　　　　　　　B. Smart phones.
　　　　C. Taxis.　　　　　　　　　　D. Modern technologies.

(　　)52. The underlined word "convenient" in Paragraph 2 is closest in meaning to "_____".
　　　　A. useful　　B. normal　　C. suitable　　D. easy

(　　)53. Compared to traditional city facilities, smart systems do better in _____.
　　　　A. detecting water　　　　　　B. supplying water
　　　　C. producing water　　　　　　D. saving water

(　　)54. The example of Santander shows the use of smart systems in aspects(方面) EXCEPT _____.
　　　　A. business　　　　　　　　　B. health care
　　　　C. traffic controlling　　　　　D. public transportation

(　　)55. What's the main idea of the passage?
　　　　A. Digital technologies help improve city planning.
　　　　B. Smart cities will make our future life better and easier.
　　　　C. Smart cities are very common in both Dubuque and Santander.
　　　　D. Spain and the US take the leading position in building smart cities.

第二节　词义搭配：从(B)栏中选出(A)栏单词的正确解释。(共10分,每小题1分)

　　　　(A)　　　　　　　　　　　　(B)

(　　)56. creativity　　　A. an occupation, such as law, medicine, that requires a lot of training and specialised study

(　　)57. imaginative　　B. the conditions or scenery around a person or place

(　　)58. profession　　　C. the ability to invent

(　　)59. influence　　　D. having a lively imagination, especially creative

(　　)60. surroundings　　E. to change the behavior or thinking of (someone)

(　　)61. moreover　　　F. want to know something surprising

(　　)62. convenience　　G. besides, what is more

Unit 1 A Small Change Can Solve the Problems of Many

(   )63. curious   H. convenient for sb

(   )64. donate   I. a bag to store letters

(   )65. envelope   J. give for free for some use

第三节 补全对话:根据对话内容,从对话后的选项中选出能填入空白处的最佳选项。(共10分,每小题2分)

A: Mike, you look worried. __66__

B: I got up late again this morning. And my teacher was a little bit angry. What could I do?

A: __67__

B: Of course, I did. But actually, I always shut it off when it rings.

A: I have a good idea. __68__ And when it rings, you have to get up and shut it off.

B: It's great. But I'm afraid I need some special alarm clocks to wake me up. __69__

A: Sure, I have made some creative alarm clocks in our school club. __70__ Let me introduce some to you.

B. It's so kind of you. Thank you.

> A. They really works.
> B. You can put your alarm clock far from you bed.
> C. What's up?
> D. Have you known such special alarm clocks?
> E. Did you set an alarm on your clock?

第三部分 语言技能应用(共分四节,满分30分)

第一节 单词拼写:根据下列句子及所给汉语注释,在横线上写出该单词。(共5分,每小题1分)

71. Could you tell me how you sealed the _____ (信封)?

72. I believe we are all _____ (有创造力的) by nature.

73. Creative people pay more attention to their _____ (周围的事物).

74. We are all _____ (影响) by things around us and things we have been exposed to.

75. A small change can _____ (解决) the problems of many.

第二节 词形变换:用括号内单词的适当形式填空,将正确答案写在横线上。(共5分,每小题1分)

76. If it is a legal matter, you need to seek _____ (profession) advice.

77. With your _____ (permit), I would like to visit the institute.

78. If you hear the _____ (continue) fire alarm, you must leave the building by the

— 17 —

nearest exit.

79. Human beings are different from animals, because they can _____ (inventive) more and more tools and machines.

80. Reading books can _____ (broad) one's mind.

第三节 改错：从 A、B、C、D 四个画线处找出一处有错误的选项，并写出正确答案。（共 10 分，每小题 2 分）

81. Creative people pay great attention to things around them.
    　　A　　　　　　B　　　C　　　　D

82. Stop global warming, better later than never.
    　A　　B　　　　　C　　　D

83. She gave us a description of that had happened.
    　　　A　　　　　B　　　　C　　D

84. Tell me how did you insert it into the lock.
    　A　　　B　　　　　C　　D

85. She asked me what some eggs floated in water and others sank.
    　　　　A　　B　　　　　　C　　　　　　　　D

81.(　)应为_____ 82.(　)应为_____ 83.(　)应为_____
84.(　)应为_____ 85.(　)应为_____

第四节 书面表达。（共 10 分）

请写一篇"创新"为主题的文章，介绍创新的重要性和如何培养创新能力，字数 60~80 字，首句已提供，不计入字数。

内容提示：

1. 创新有助于解决问题。富有创新的人具有开放和活跃的思维，他们总是寻找新的方式解决问题，这能激发创新并提高效率。

2. 给自己一些时间放松或玩耍，也许当散步或洗澡的时候，你就突然想到了一个好主意。

3. 创新鼓励多提问。当你需要寻求一个解决办法时，问自己尽可能多的问题，只要头脑风暴一下，你就会找到好方法。

Creativity is important not only to individuals but also to our nation.

Unit 2

It's Always Nice to Be Polite

Warming up

一、句型总结

1. I'm busy preparing for an internship. 我正忙着为实习做准备呢。

2. Actually, I'm quite anxious about how I'll do. 事实上,我很担心我该怎么做。

3. But if you do make an effort during the internship, things will work out. 但如果你在实习期间努力,就一定没问题的。

4. I think you need to pay attention to different rules of etiquette. 我认为你需要注意不同的礼仪规则。

5. Dress smartly to make a good impression. Avoid wearing heavy make-up and strong perfume. 得体的着装会给人留下好印象。避免化浓妆或用浓烈的香水。

6. I'll keep your advice in mind. 我会记住你的建议。

7. I really recognise the importance of etiquette. 我真的认识到了礼仪的重要性。

8. I forgot to turn off my mobile phone and it rang during a meeting. 我忘记关手机了,而且手机在会议期间响了。

9. Following the rules of etiquette can help us perform well in the workplace. 遵守礼仪规则可以帮助我们在职场中表现得更好。

10. A survey says most workers get a B when it comes to good behaviour in the workplace. 一项调查显示,大多数职员在职场行为得体方面只能得 B。

11. You need to show your respect for your colleagues. 你需要表示出对你的同事的尊重。

12. This promotion brings me a feeling of joy and responsibility. 这次提升给我带来了快乐感和责任感。

13. I shall do my best to perform my duties, and try to be worthy of your wishes. 我将尽力履行好我的职责,并尽力去对得起你的祝福。

二、英汉互译

1. 直挺地_____
2. (业务)名片_____
3. 准时的、守时的_____
4. 愿考虑不同意见的,思想开明的_____
5. 实习(期)_____
6. 化妆_____
7. 礼节、礼仪、规矩_____
8. 顺利地_____
9. 尴尬的_____
10. 不合适的、不得体的_____

Listening and Speaking

一、找出与所给单词画线部分读音相同的选项

( ) 1. g<u>e</u>sture   A. r<u>e</u>cognize   B. stat<u>e</u>ment   C. <u>e</u>mergency   D. r<u>e</u>minder

( ) 2. sh<u>a</u>ke   A. h<u>a</u>nd   B. <u>a</u>ctive   C. <u>a</u>bsent   D. m<u>a</u>ke

( ) 3. p<u>u</u>nctual   A. <u>u</u>pright   B. b<u>u</u>siness   C. b<u>u</u>sy   D. <u>u</u>seful

( ) 4. p<u>o</u>lite   A. <u>o</u>pen   B. h<u>o</u>ld   C. c<u>o</u>de   D. c<u>o</u>ngratulations

( ) 5. w<u>ear</u>   A. h<u>ear</u>   B. p<u>ear</u>   C. h<u>ear</u>d   D. f<u>ear</u>

二、从 B 栏中找出与 A 栏中相对应的答语

A	B
1. What was Li Li doing? 2. What should I wear for the job interview? 3. What are you busy with? 4. You must have learnt a lesson anyhow. 5. What should I pay attention to?	A. You should wear a suit and tie for the job interview. B. Li Li was sitting upright in her chair. C. I've got an internship for this summer, so I'm busy preparing for it. D. I think you need to pay attention to different rules of etiquette. E. Certainly! I really recognise the importance of etiquette.

1. _____   2. _____   3. _____   4. _____   5. _____

三、补全对话

A：Hi, Tom. You look upset today. What's up?

B：Hi, James. I'm nervous about my coming internship as a receptionist.

A：__1__ You've been trained for it for a long time.

B：I know that but I'm not confident at all. __2__

A：There is no need to suffer from imaginary fears. __3__

B：What should I pay attention to?

A：As a receptionist, it's important to make a good impression. __4__

B：Thanks for your advice.

A：That's all right. __5__

> A. I'm afraid I would make mistakes.
> B. Take it easy.
> C. I bet you will perform well.
> D. Everything will go smoothly if you follow several basic rules.
> E. Dress smartly, wear smiles, use polite language and things will work out.

四、情景模拟(主题对话)

编写一组对话。

List more examples of improper workplace behaviors and give suggestions accordingly.

_____
_____
_____
_____
_____
_____

Reading and Writing

一、用所给词的适当形式填空

1. When _____ (step) into an office, you should try to observe the things on the board.

2. Turn the air conditioner off when you leave or it will be _____（exhaust）tomorrow.

3. The purpose of the _____（remind）on the coffee desk is so obvious that all the employees understand it immediately.

4. Take a deep _____（breathe）before you send an e-mail to your boss.

5. She created so many spectacular products for the company that she was soon promoted to chief _____（design）.

6. I believe you learnt a lot during the _____（实习期）.

7. Pay attention to your _____（手势），when you speak to the public.

8. Be _____（准时），when you go to the interview.

9. _____（恭喜），you have passed the exam.

10. Choose the most important qualities for a new _____（雇员）.

二、完形填空

A true apology is more than just acknowledgment（承认）of a mistake. It's recognition that something you've said or done has damaged a relationship—and that you care enough about that relationship to want it 1 .

It's never 2 to acknowledge you are in the wrong. Being human, we all need the art of apology. Look back and think how often you've judged roughly, said   3   things, pushed yourself ahead at the expense of a friend. Some deep thought lets us know that when   4   a small mistake has been made, your feeling will stay out of balance until the mistake is acknowledged and your regret is 5 .

I remember a doctor friend, telling me about a man who came to him with   6   illnesses: headache, insomnia, stomachaches and so on. No physical cause could be found. Finally the doctor said to the man, " 7   you tell me what's on your conscience, I can't help you."

After a short silence, the man told the doctor that he seize all the money that his father gave to his brother, who was   8 . His father had died, so only he himself knew the matter. The doctor made the man write to his brother making an   9   and enclosing a check. In the post office, the man dropped the letter into the mail box. As the letter disappeared, the man burst into tears."Thank you, doctor," he said, "I think I'm all right now." And he   10 .

( )1. A. built   B. formed   C. repaired   D. damaged
( )2. A. difficult   B. easy   C. foolish   D. shy
( )3. A. unusual   B. harmful   C. worthless   D. unkind
( )4. A. hardly   B. even   C. only   D. such
( )5. A. apologized   B. explained   C. offered   D. expressed

Unit 2   It's Always Nice to Be Polite

(   )6. A. strange   B. fatal   C. various   D. dangerous
(   )7. A. Whenever   B. Unless   C. Suppose   D. Although
(   )8. A. mad   B. lost   C. abroad   D. dead
(   )9. A. order   B. excuse   C. agreement   D. apology
(   )10. A. should   B. did   C. had   D. was

三、阅读理解

阅读下面短文,从每题所给的 A、B、C、D 四个选项中选出最佳答案。

When people meet each other for the first time in Britain, they say "How do you do?" and shake hands(握手). Usually they do not shake hands when they just meet or say goodbye. But they shake hands after they haven't met for a long time or when they will be away from each other for a long time.

Last year a group of German students went to England for a holiday. Their teacher told them that the English people hardly shake hands. So when they met their English friends at the station, they kept their hands behind their backs. The English students had learned that the Germans shake hands as often as possible, so they put their hands in front and got ready to shake hands with them. It made both of them laugh.

(   )1. It is _____ if you know the language and some of the customs of the country.
   A. not useful   B. not helpful   C. very helpful   D. very bad

(   )2. English people usually shake hands when they _____.
   A. meet every time   B. meet for the first time
   C. say goodbye to each other   D. say hello to each other

(   )3. Usually English people don't shake hands _____.
   A. when they will be away for a long time
   B. when they say "How do you do?"
   C. when they just meet or say goodbye
   D. after they haven't met for a long time

(   )4. Which is right?
   A. German people shake hands as often as possible.
   B. English people like shaking hands very much.
   C. German people hardly shake hands.
   D. Neither English people nor Germans like shaking hands.

(   )5. This story is about _____.
   A. shaking hands   B. languages
   C. customs   D. languages and customs

— 23 —

四、书面表达

以"My advice on internship etiquette"为题,写一篇文章,字数 80~100 字.

Grammar

一、从下面每小题四个选项中选出最佳选项

(　　)1. Our Chinese teacher didn't go to bed _____ he finished his work last night.
   A. if   B. until   C. since   D. because

(　　)2. We will put off the picnic in the park until next week, _____ the weather may be better.
   A. that   B. where   C. which   D. when

(　　)3. The farmer watered the vegetables in the field _____ they might grow better.
   A. in case   B. for fear that   C. in order   D. so that

(　　)4. I won't accept their offer, _____ favorable the conditions are.
   A. how   B. however   C. no matter   D. no matter however

(　　)5. _____ it happened to be a nice day, we decided to go to the beach.
   A. When   B. Before   C. If   D. Since

(　　)6. We were just about ready to leave _____ it started to snow.
   A. when   B. before   C. after   D. since

(　　)7. I'll keep his address _____ I need it.
   A. so that   B. in order that   C. in case   D. when

(　　)8. Will you keep my place in the queue for me _____ I go and make a phone call?
   A. since   B. while   C. in case   D. until

(　　)9. The fire went on for quite some time _____ it was brought under control.
   A. when   B. since   C. after   D. before

Unit 2 It's Always Nice to Be Polite

(　　)10. _____ I suggest, he always disagrees.

　　A. However　　B. Whatever　　C. Whichever　　D. Whoever

(　　)11. _____ the government agrees to give extra money, the theater will have to close.

　　A. Until　　B. Unless　　C. Since　　D. While

(　　)12. Their country has plenty of oil _____ ours has none.

　　A. while　　B. when　　C. unless　　D. since

(　　)13. You should let your children play _____ you can see them.

　　A. where　　B. when　　C. in which　　D. that

(　　)14. They kept trying _____ they must have known it was hopeless.

　　A. if　　B. because　　C. when　　D. where

(　　)15. _____ I do for her, she never feels happy.

　　A. Whichever　　B. Whatever　　C. However　　D. Whenever

(　　)16. You can't park your car _____ you like because it will bring trouble to others.

　　A. wherever　　B. whatever　　C. whether　　D. whichever

(　　)17. —Why didn't he pass the exam?

　　—_____ he didn't study hard.

　　A. Because　　B. As　　C. Since　　D. For

(　　)18. I'll stay here _____ everyone else comes back.

　　A. even if　　B. as though　　C. because　　D. until

(　　)19. _____ the day went on, the weather got worse.

　　A. With　　B. Since　　C. While　　D. As

(　　)20. _____ the movie may be, we have no time to see it.

　　A. Although exciting　　B. No matter exciting

　　C. Whatever exciting　　D. However exciting

(　　)21. We had no sooner got to the station _____ the train left.

　　A. when　　B. than　　C. after　　D. before

(　　)22. _____ poor, we are proud of our mother.

　　A. When　　B. Because　　C. Though　　D. As

(　　)23. I'll go _____ they invite me.

　　A. though　　B. unless　　C. as　　D. as long as

(　　)24. It is about ten years _____ I met you last time.

　　A. since　　B. for　　C. when　　D. as

(　　)25. Clever _____ he is, he sometimes makes mistakes.

　　A. as　　B. when　　C. since　　D. for

(   )26. He walked down the dark street _____ he feared no danger.
　　　　A. so that　　　B. as if　　　C. unless　　　D. until

(   )27. He will come to call on you the moment he _____ his painting.
　　　　A. will finish　　B. finishes　　C. has finished　　D. had finished

(   )28. _____ he is old, but he works just as hard as everyone else.
　　　　A. Although　　B. Because　　C. /　　D. Unless

(   )29. He studies very hard _____ he can pass the exam.
　　　　A. such that　　B. in order that　　C. in order to　　D. so as to

(   )30. King _____ he is, he is unhappy.
　　　　A. because　　B. so　　C. if　　D. as

二、找出下列句子中错误的选项，并改正过来

1. Whatever difficult the task may be, we will try our best to complete it on time.
   　A　　　　　　　　　　　　B　　　　　C　　　　　　　　　　　　D

2. We had hardly left the building than it fell down.
   　　　A　　B　　　　　　　　C　　D

3. She liked the ancient Chinese vase too much that she would like to take it.
   　　　A　　　　B　　　　　　C　　　　　　　　　D

4. If he is awake or asleep, the subject is always in his mind.
   A　　　B　　C　　　　　　　　　　　　　D

5. I'll let you know as soon as he will come back.
   　A　　　　B　　　C　　　D

6. You can't borrow books from the school library after you get your student card.
   　　　　A　　　　B　　　　　　　　　　C　　　D

7. As though the forest park is far away, a lot of tourists visit it every year.
   　A　　　　　　　　　　　　B　　　　　　　C　　　D

8. Today, we will begin that we stopped yesterday so that no point will be left out.
   　　　　A　　　B　　　　　　　　　　　　C　　　　　　　D

9. Studying in groups is necessary though you want to do well in school.
   　A　　　　B　　　　　　　　　C　　　　　　D

10. It was such a lovely weather that they decided to spend the day in the park.
    　　　A　　　　　　　B　　　C　　　　D

More Activities

一、找出与所给单词画线部分读音相同的选项

(   )1. smoothly　　A. good　　B. cooking　　C. food　　D. booklet

Unit 2　It's Always Nice to Be Polite

(　　)2. properly　　A. colleague　　B. confuse　　C. tone　　D. zero

(　　)3. manner　　A. master　　B. behaviour　　C. statement　　D. attitude

(　　)4. frighten　　A. attitude　　B. reminder　　C. ignore　　D. switch

(　　)5. anyhow　　A. growth　　B. crowd　　C. flow　　D. owner

二、汉译英

1. 职场行为_____

2. 走进办公室_____

3. 在告示板上_____

4. 对……有把握_____

5. 去一个安静的角落_____

6. 打电话_____

7. 把……放回到架子上_____

8. 关闭……（电器）_____

9. 深呼吸_____

10. 设计一些告示语_____

三、用所给单词的适当形式填空

1. A survey says most workers get a B when it comes to good _____ (behave) in the workplace.

2. If it is an _____ (emergent), be sure to tell the attendees beforehand.

3. Did everything go _____ (smooth) with your internship?

4. I really realized the _____ (important) of punctuality.

5. But I also made an _____ (embarrass) mistake.

6. You need to show your respect for your _____ (colleague).

7. It's a small _____ (formal) party—you don't have to dress up.

8. He has _____ (master) the rules of business etiquette.

9. Read the following _____ (reminder)—do you understand them?

10. Ever wonder why people don't _____ (response) to your emails?

四、找出下列句子中错误的选项，并改正过来

1. Unless you don't explain clearly, you'll just confuse the readers.
　　A　　　　B　　　　C　　　　　　　　　　　　D

2. After I could say anything more, he had left.
　　A　　B　　　C　　　　　　D

3. He is too busy that he can't help me with my English.
　　　A　　B　　C　　　　D

4. I was doing my homework while suddenly he came.
　　A　　　　B　　　　C　　　　　D

5. As long as you will stick to the end, you are sure to succeed.
　　A　　　　B　　　C　　　　　　　　　D

单元检测

第一部分 英语知识运用(共分三节,满分40分)

第一节 语音知识:从 A、B、C、D 四个选项中找出其画线部分与所给单词画线部分读音相同的选项。(共5分,每小题1分)

( )1. man<u>n</u>ers   A. co<u>n</u>fuse   B. <u>s</u>ummary   C. fal<u>s</u>e   D. di<u>s</u>count

( )2. smoo<u>th</u>ly   A. brea<u>th</u>   B. heal<u>th</u>   C. weal<u>th</u>   D. ba<u>th</u>e

( )3. sh<u>e</u>lf   A. stat<u>e</u>ment   B. qu<u>e</u>ue   C. dr<u>e</u>ss   D. b<u>e</u>haviour

( )4. s<u>u</u>mmary   A. conf<u>u</u>se   B. calc<u>u</u>lator   C. val<u>u</u>e   D. p<u>u</u>nctual

( )5. <u>i</u>nternship   A. <u>i</u>gnore   B. <u>i</u>sland   C. fr<u>i</u>ghten   D. l<u>i</u>ghted

第二节 词汇与语法知识:从 A、B、C、D 四个选项中选出可以填入空白处的最佳选项。(共25分,每小题1分)

( )6. Members and their _____ from work meet at the park for outdoor games.
    A. colleges   B. classmates   C. colleagues   D. parent

( )7. The job is great in _____ of salary, but it has its disadvantages.
    A. terms   B. matter   C. case   D. language

( )8. Don't expect anything original from him. He just goes with the _____! Which following word CAN'T fit into the blank?
    A. flow   B. crowd   C. public   D. student

( )9. All the little girls in the neighbourhood _____ as angels for the coming festival.
    A. dress up   B. dress down   C. get up   D. dressing

( )10. _____ sure to give your family my regards.
    A. Make   B. Do   C. Be   D. May

( )11. We know we should cut down on fat but that doesn't help when it comes _____ eating.
    A. on   B. to   C. at   D. with

( )12. Jacky has worked _____ hard to get into this position and he wants to hang on to it.
    A. extremely   B. too   C. a bit   D. so

( )13. Bobby had absolutely no _____, speaking with his mouth full and his _____ on the table.
    A. workplace etiquette; hands   B. table manners; elbows

Unit 2　It's Always Nice to Be Polite

　　　　C. basic rules；mobile phone　　　D. manners；head

(　)14. The stepmother told one of her two daughters to cut off her big toe to _____ the shoe.

　　　　A. fit into　　　B. step into　　　C. break into　　　D. divide into

(　)15. We should _____ people who have different values in the workplace.

　　　　A. show our respect for　　　B. disrespect for

　　　　C. get away from　　　D. hate into

(　)16. The CEO sent a _____ to all staff that company resources are only for company use.

　　　　A. notice　　　B. reminder　　　C. bill　　　D. words

(　)17. This was the moment when Neil Armstrong became the first man to step _____ the moon.

　　　　A. into　　　B. down　　　C. on　　　D. up

(　)18. The way to tell if your pets are unhealthy is to _____ their behaviour.

　　　　A. observe　　　B. see　　　C. look　　　D. notice

(　)19. Anyone who goes shopping without a list is _____ to forget the things they really need.

　　　　A. sure　　　B. impossible　　　C. expected　　　D. intended

(　)20. —Mark, the phone is ringing. My hands are full. Please _____ it for me.

　　　　—Sure, Mum.

　　　　A. take　　　B. make　　　C. hang　　　D. put

(　)21. The unexpected sad news upsets and _____ George's family.

　　　　A. excites　　　B. disturbs　　　C. surprises　　　D. make

(　)22. It was getting dark inside my room. I forced myself to get up from my chair and _____ some lights.

　　　　A. put on　　　B. turn down　　　C. turn on　　　D. take off

(　)23. He was so _____ that he fell asleep at his desk.

　　　　A. exhausted　　　B. excited　　　C. worried　　　D. surprised

(　)24. He was so talkative that he spoke for one and a half hours and barely paused to _____ .

　　　　A. breathed　　　B. take a breath　　　C. breath　　　D. breathing

(　)25. Some children keep attractive cards in an album as a constant _____ of their grandparents.

　　　　A. reminder　　　B. memory　　　C. remember　　　D. thing

(　)26. If you don't _____ to the point quickly then you may lose their interest halfway through the email.

  A. get   B. move   C. run   D. sit

( )27. We are unwilling to risk _____ any client as we try to get our business back to normal.

  A. lose   B. to lose   C. losing   D. lost

( )28. Although the dress code in our company is a little lengthy, I will try to explain it as _____ as possible.

  A. shortly   B. concisely   C. complicated   D. long

( )29. Police are warning the public to be on the alert for _____ packages.

  A. suspicious   B. surprising   C. sudden   D. pick

( )30. The best way to respond _____ spam mails is to ignore them.

  A. to   B. by   C. with   D. for

第三节　完形填空：阅读下面的短文，从所给的 A、B、C、D 四个选项中选出最佳的答案。(共 10 分，每小题 1 分)

  Arabs（阿拉伯人）consider it extremely bad manners to start talking business immediately. __31__ the busiest government official always takes extra time to be polite and offer refreshments（茶点）. No matter how busy you are, you should make time for this hospitality（好客）.

  The "conference visit" is a way of doing __32__ throughout the Arab world. Frequently, you will have to discuss your business in the presence of strangers. Do not be __33__ if your meeting is interrupted several times by people who come into the room unannounced（突然地、未通知地）, speak softly to the person with whom you are __34__, and leave. Act as though you do not hear, and never show displeasure at being interrupted.

  Making decisions quickly is not an Arab custom. There is a vagueness（模糊）in doing business in the Middle East which will __35__ a newcomer. Give yourself lots of time and ask lots of questions.

  __36__ is an important quality. You may have to wait two or three days to see high-level government officials as they are very busy. Give yourself enough __37__.

  Personal relationships are very __38__. They are the key to doing business in Arab countries. Try to identify the decision-maker and get to __39__ him. Do your homework. Be prepared to discuss details of your __40__ or service. Be ready to answer technical questions.

( )31. A. Also   B. Even   C. Only   D. Still

( )32. A. good   B. homework   C. work   D. business

( )33. A. surprised   B. pleased   C. embarrassed   D. scared

( )34. A. eating   B. chatting   C. talking   D. quarreling

( )35. A. interest   B. puzzle   C. attract   D. prove

Unit 2　It's Always Nice to Be Polite

(　　)36. A. Patience　　　B. Politeness　　　C. Hospitality　　　D. Kindness

(　　)37. A. time　　　　B. room　　　　　C. space　　　　　D. money

(　　)38. A. tense　　　　B. important　　　C. common　　　　D. open

(　　)39. A. know　　　　B. introduce　　　C. contact　　　　D. forget

(　　)40. A. decision　　　B. product　　　　C. talk　　　　　D. identity

第二部分　篇章与词汇理解(共分三节,满分 50 分)

第一节　阅读理解:阅读下列短文,从每题所给的 A、B、C、D 四个选项中选出最恰当的答案。(共 30 分,每小题 2 分)

A

Having good etiquette at the workplace is very important to be a favourite in an office. However, it's observed that many people aren't aware of workplace etiquette and this creates a very bad impression in the office. So it's important to know some workplace etiquette tips.

Among all the workplace etiquette guidelines, the most important is to be punctual. Though going late due to an emergency is okay, habitual latecomers are never appreciated in any organization. Arriving at your office on time shows that you're aware of your responsibilities and have respect for the organization. In case you feel that you would be late, call and report the matter to the concerned authority.

Also, a proper knowledge of workplace email etiquette is a must. In the official emails, you need to mention the subject concisely, and at the same time include all the important details which are to be shared. You should use good and grammatically correct language while writing emails.

Knowledge of telephone etiquette in the workplace is very important as well. While talking on the telephone, be polite and listen to what they're saying carefully. Only then should you say what you feel. Speak in a voice which would be heard clearly at the other end.

The workplace guidelines are important even while you're dining or celebrating with your co-workers. If you get a call in between, receive it after you're permitted by the others by saying "excuse me". Don't talk loudly while eating. Greet people well and try to make them feel comfortable.

These guidelines will help you become the best employee of a company.

(　　)41. The intended readers of the passage are _____.

A. managers in charge of a company

B. students of a business class

C. people who are out of work

D. general readers

(　　)42. Why should you try to be punctual?

A. To prove you are not a habitual latecomer.

B. To respect the rules of the organization.

C. To show that you are a responsible worker.

D. To win other workers' respect.

( )43. How should you write an official email?

A. Write the subject clearly and simply.

B. Include all the details in the email.

C. Make the language as beautiful as possible.

D. Make emails as brief as possible.

( )44. Which of the following is considered NOT acceptable about making phone calls?

A. Using polite languages.

B. Listening with patience and care.

C. Speaking clearly.

D. Answering a call whenever it comes in.

( )45. In the writer's opinion, workplace etiquette _____.

A. is easy to master

B. is considered important by all employees

C. can be helpful in doing your work well

D. will bring you good luck and good salaries

B

American people like to say "Thank you" when others help them or say something kind to them. People of many countries do so, too. It is a very good habit.

You should say "Thank you" when someone passes you the salt on the table, when someone walking ahead of you keeps the door open for you, when someone says you have done your work well, or you have bought a nice thing, or your city is very beautiful. "Thank you" is used not only between friends, but also between parents and children, brothers and sisters.

"Excuse me" is another short sentence they use. When you hear someone say so behind you, you know that somebody wants to walk past you without touching you. It's not polite to break others when they are talking. If you want to speak to one of them, say "Excuse me" first, and then begin talking. You should also do so when you begin to cough or make any noise before others.

( )46. You should say "Thank you" when _____.

A. you say something kind to others   B. you help others

C. someone helps you   D. you need others to help you

( )47. From the passage we know "Thank you" is _____.

A. widely used in the world

Unit 2　It's Always Nice to Be Polite

B. used more often than "Excuse me"

C. used only by Americans

D. used only between friends

(　　)48. You should say "Excuse me" if you want to _____.

A. leave someone　　　　　B. thank someone

C. help someone　　　　　D. make some noise

(　　)49. When you are going to ask someone to tell you the way, you should say "_____".

A. Thank you　　　　　B. That's very kind of you

C. Excuse me　　　　　D. I'm sorry

(　　)50. This passage mainly tells us the way _____.

A. to be happy　　　　　B. to be polite

C. to help others　　　　D. to learn more from Americans

C

Some British and American people like to invite friends and colleagues for a meal at home. You should not be upset (心烦意乱) if your English friends don't invite you home. It doesn't mean they don't like you.

Dinner parties usually start between 7:00 and 8:00 p.m., and end at about 11:00 p.m. Ask your hosts what time you should arrive. It's polite to bring flowers, chocolates or a bottle of wine as a present.

Do you want to be extra (特别地) polite? Say how much you like the room, or the pictures on the wall. But remember not to ask how much things cost.

You'll probably start the meal with soup, or something small as a "starter" (开胃小吃), then you'll have meat or fish with vegetables, and then a dessert (甜食), followed by coffee. It's polite to finish everything on your plate and to take more if you want it. Some people eat bread with their meal, but not everyone does.

Before they take out their cigarettes after the meal, most people usually ask, "Do you mind if I smoke here?"

Did you enjoy the evening? Call your hosts the next day, or write them a short "Thank you" letter. Perhaps it seems funny to you but British and American people say, "thank you, thank you, and thank you" all the time.

(　　)51. If your English or American friends don't invite you to dinner at home, _____.

A. it shows they don't like you

B. it shows they have no time to get together

C. it shows they don't want to make friends with you

D. it doesn't show they don't like you

( )52. When you are invited to go to your friend's home, _____.

A. you shouldn't take anything with you

B. you may go at any time

C. you may take an expensive present with you

D. you may take a small present with you

( )53. In England and America, it's not polite to _____.

A. ask the price of a thing   B. eat all the food on your plate

C. talk to your hosts   D. eat too fast

( )54. In the passage, the order of the serving of a meal is _____.

A. dessert-meat or fish with vegetables-coffee-soup

B. coffee-soup-dessert-meat or fish with vegetables

C. meat or fish with vegetables-dessert-soup-coffee

D. soup-meat or fish with vegetables-dessert-coffee

( )55. Which of the following is NOT right?

A. In England or America, it usually takes more than three hours to have a dinner party at home.

B. If you are invited to go to a dinner party, you can't arrive early.

C. You mustn't smoke after a meal when you are with some American or English people.

D. You'd better write a short "Thank you" letter to your hosts or give them a call if you want to be extra polite.

第二节 词义搭配:从(B)栏中选出(A)栏单词的正确解释。(共10分,每小题1分)

(A)　　　　　　　　　　(B)

( )56. emergency   A. behaviour that is considered to be polite in a particular society or culture

( )57. manner   B. beliefs about what is right and wrong and what is important in life

( )58. values   C. a sudden serious and dangerous event or situation which needs immediate action to deal with

( )59. beforehand   D. to take somebody's attention away from what they are trying to do

( )60. distract   E. earlier; before something else happens or is done

( )61. colleague   F. know something thoroughly

( )62. master   G. correctly, suitably

( )63. behaviour   H. one person who works together with you

( )64. properly   I. actions or things one person behaves

( )65. recognise   J. know something / someone you know before

第三节　补全对话:根据对话内容,从对话后的选项中选出能填入空白处的最佳选项。(共 10 分,每小题 2 分)

A: Carter, you seem extremely upset. What happened?

B: I'm so worried about the email I just sent to one of my colleagues in IT department. I hope it won't cause any trouble.

A: What's wrong with the email?

B: __66__ I asked my colleague about a computer glitch via email but I sent it to the whole IT department and even my boss!

A: __67__

B: What's worse, there are many wrong spellings, suspicious links and unspecified attachments in that email.

A: Oh, that really seems unprofessional.

B: Yes, __68__ right now. I should have learned about it more carefully.

A: __69__ It's really important to proofread and check the recipients before sending emails.

B: Definitely. __70__

> A. I really recognise the importance of email etiquette.
> B. What an awkward moment!
> C. Don't mention it.
> D. I couldn't agree more.
> E. I have already learned my lesson.

第三部分　语言技能应用(共分四节,满分 30 分)

第一节　单词拼写:根据下列句子及所给汉语注释,在横线上写出该单词。(共 5 分,每小题 1 分)

71. I'm nervous about my coming _____ (实习期) as a receptionist.

72. It's important to make a good _____ (印象) on your boss.

73. Can you list more good workplace _____ (举止,行为).

74. I really _____ (认识到) the importance of email etiquette.

75. As a translator you should _____ (掌握) two languages at least.

第二节　词形变换:用括号内单词的适当形式填空,将正确答案写在横线上。(共 5 分,每小题 1 分)

76. You mean dress code and _____ (punctual)?

77. You should accept a business card _____ (proper).

78. You will perform and _____ (behaviour) well in the workplace.

79. At the end of the speech, he made a _____ (summarize).

80. You nearly _____ (fright) me to death.

第三节 改错：从 A、B、C、D 四个画线处找出一处有错误的选项，并写出正确答案。（共 10 分，每小题 2 分）

81. A briefly summary of this article is given here.
   A   B   C   D

82. Please go to a quiet corner to make a call, or your colleagues may be disturbe.
     A   B   C   D

83. Read the following reminder—do you understand them?
   A   B   C   D

84. People don't want their email addresses shared so wide.
   A   B   C D

85. If some extra money is found, the factory will close.
  A   B   C   D

81.（ ）应为_____ 82.（ ）应为_____ 83.（ ）应为_____

84.（ ）应为_____ 85.（ ）应为_____

第四节 书面表达。（共 10 分）

86. 请写一篇以"职场礼仪"为主题的文章，为职场新人介绍必备的职场礼仪贴士和建议，字数 60~80 字，首句已提供，不计入字数。

内容提示：

1. 尽快融入企业文化。熟记并严格遵守公司的规章制度，不迟到早退、办公时间不打私人电话；

2. 从小事做起。多做一些力所能及的琐事，如为复印机加纸，给饮水机（water dispenser）加水等，它们能给人留下好印象；

3. 虚心请教同事。问问题是解决问题、增加沟通、增进情谊的有效手段。

Workplace Etiquette Tips

  Workplace etiquette is increasingly important and influences people's career success. Here are some useful etiquette tips for those who just start out in their career.

Unit 3

We Are Part of Nature

Warming up

一、句型总结

1. I do two things to celebrate. First, I observe a zero carbon day.我做两件事来庆祝。首先,我过一个零碳日。

2. Planting a tree is a lot of fun, as well as helping the environment.种树很有趣,也利于保护环境。

3. Our kitchen is equipped with A-rated fridges.我们的厨房配备了A级冰箱。

4. "A-rated" means they are very efficient and they don't use much electricity."A级"意味着它们省电、高效。

5. And you might even catch sight of a rabbit.你甚至会瞥见兔子的身影。

6. All living things work together to keep a prairie ecosystem healthy.所有生物共同协作以保持草原生态系统的健康。

7. These species might not survive in a different ecosystem.这些物种在不同的生态系统中可能无法生存。

8. A healthy ecosystem is essential for the survival of all living things.一个健康的生态系统对所有生物的存活是至关重要的。

9. Low-carbon living means a type of lifestyle in which people do their best to reduce energy consumption and carbon emissions. 低碳生活是指人们尽最大努力减少能源消耗和碳排放的一种生活方式。

10. A low-carbon lifestyle contributes a lot to environmental protection and it is a good way of slowing down climate change. 低碳的生活方式对环境保护有巨大贡献,是减缓气候变化的好方法。

11. We should develop good habits in our daily life。我们应该在日常生活中养成良好的习惯。

12. And lights should be turned off if not needed. This greatly reduces electricity consumption. 如果不需要用灯,我们应随手关灯。这会大大减少电力消耗。

二、英汉互译

1. 本地农产品_____
2. 垃圾_____
3. 公共交通_____
4. 包装;外包装_____
5. 可回收利用的_____
6. 能源消耗(量)_____
7. 策略;政策_____
8. 高效能的;有效率的_____
9. 餐具_____
10. 打折_____

Listening and Speaking

一、找出与所给单词画线部分读音相同的选项

(　　) 1. ecosystem　　A. local　　　B. policy　　C. confuse　　D. colleagues

(　　) 2. recyclable　　A. energy　　B. policy　　C. beauty　　D. apply

(　　) 3. celebrate　　A. reporter　　B. efficient　　C. beneath　　D. eggplant

(　　) 4. discount　　A. coupon　　B. outbreak　　C. generous　　D. trouble

(　　) 5. link　　　　A. sink　　　B. contain　　C. carbon　　D. efficient

Unit 3 We Are Part of Nature

二、从 B 栏中找出与 A 栏中相对应的答语

A

1. Sorting the daily waste
2. Walking to work
3. Buying second-hand goods
4. Taking short showers
5. Avoiding buying bottled water

B

A. It reduces water waste and helps you save money. It also reduces the packaging waste that contains toxic chemicals.

B. It reduces and saves gallons of water for both your family and the country.

C. It helps turn waste into treasure and save resources. It brings great economic benefits to the country and reduces environmental pollution.

D. It saves you lots of money and helps protect the environment and preserve natural resources by minimum packaging.

E. It helps the city reduce air pollution and traffic jams. It saves you on transportation costs and helps you maintain a healthy body and mind.

1. _____ 2. _____ 3. _____ 4. _____ 5. _____

三、补全对话

A：Hi, Jessie. Have you heard that new waste-sorting rules are in place in our city to help protect the environment?

B：Yes, Mike. Actually, I'm busy learning the rules these days.

A：Really? __1__

B：Generally speaking, we need to divide daily rubbish into four categories: kitchen waste, recyclable waste, hazardous waste, and other waste.

A：Well, I'm not quite sure about kitchen waste or other waste. __2__

B：Kitchen waste can also be called wet waste. __3__

A：I see. __4__

B：Other waste is also called dry waste, which refers to nontoxic waste that will not rot or be recycled like used tissues.

A： __5__ Thanks for your introduction.

B：You're welcome.

> A. Could you tell me more about them?
> B. It refers to food waste that rots easily.
> C. What do we need to know about waste classification?
> D. What an expert you are!
> E. What about other waste?

四、情景模拟(主题对话)

编写一组对话,如何保护环境。

celebrate / zero carbon day / energy consumption / policy / be equipped with / efficient protect environment

_____
_____
_____
_____
_____
_____

Reading and Writing

一、用所给词的适当形式填空

1. You should talk more about _____ (environment) protection.

2. Environmentalists fear that this is a shortsighted approach to the problem of _____ (globe) warming.

3. At the factory outlet you'll find _____ (count) items at up to 75% off regular prices.

4. Schools in our city provide a variety of _____ (option) courses to cater to students of different levels.

5. Afraid of the possible economic recession, they are _____ (will) to invest more money in the project.

6. Having studied Wal-Mart's _____ (fly), she decided to buy the latest smartphone

advertised at more than 50 percent off.

7. We are proud of _____ (support) local produce.

8. "A-rated" means they are very _____ (effect) and they don't use much electricity.

9. All living things work together to keep the ecosystem _____ (health).

10. _____ (discount) vegetables and fruit options at Food Court 10 at 8 pm are available.

二、完形填空

Greenland(格陵兰岛) is the largest island in the world. It is in the north of Europe. Near Greenland is __1__ island. It is small. Its __2__ is Iceland. Do you think that Greenland is green and warm? Do you think that Iceland is white with ice? If you do, you are __3__. Not many people live on the big island of Greenland. There __4__ more people in your hometown than in all of Greenland. That is because Greenland is not green. Greenland is __5__. Most of the island is covered with lots of ice. The ice covering Greenland is __6__ than the world's tallest building. What __7__ Iceland? Is it colder than Greenland? No, it is not. Iceland has ice, but not so much ice __8__ Greenland. It has a lot of hot springs(泉). They give out hot water and steam(水蒸气). The climate(气候) is not as __9__ as Greenland. And there are a lot __10__ people who live in Iceland.

( ) 1. A. other   B. the other   C. all   D. another
( ) 2. A. village   B. name   C. farm   D. town
( ) 3. A. wrong   B. clever   C. right   D. bright
( ) 4. A. must be   B. are   C. is   D. be
( ) 5. A. yellow   B. brown   C. blue   D. white
( ) 6. A. more higher   B. high   C. highest   D. higher
( ) 7. A. of   B. in   C. about   D. on
( ) 8. A. as   B. like   C. than   D. then
( ) 9. A. warm   B. cold   C. not   D. cool
( ) 10. A. many   B. much   C. more   D. most

三、阅读理解

阅读下面短文，从每题所给的 A、B、C、D 四个选项中选出最佳答案。

A recent survey clearly reveals that the full hidden meanings of the term "global warming" are far from understood. As long as public awareness remains so low, the political measures required to deal with the disasters are unlikely to come about. Over 80 percent of the people interviewed in the survey were unable to point out any of the effects of a worldwide rise in temperature.

This is totally different from the concerns voiced by the team of professionals that conducted the survey. Team leader Professor Chang stated that we should all expect to experience great lifestyle changes as a result of the effects of global warming. In detailing the likely effects, he emphasised that the climatic changes caused by a rise in global temperature of only 1℃ would result in very big changes.

<u>Primary</u> among these changes would be the rise in sea level as a result of the melting of the polar icecaps. Although what Professor Chang said had led to a heated debate, those who share his view insist that governments must accept the challenge by investing in coastal defence. Even inland areas will not be able to avoid the effects of global warming. Changes in the rainfall pattern are likely to result in flooding and change into deserts, both of which will influence agriculture throughout the world.

In a recent interview, Professor Chang explained these points and left his audience in no doubt about the serious problem. "Unless we plan for the future, we will not encourage people to support us at local, regional, national, and international levels to face this issue — the issue of the 21st century."

(　　) 1. Global warming would have no effect on _____.
  A. agriculture   B. people's life
  C. sea level   D. political measures

(　　) 2. Who really cares about "global warming"?
  A. The government officials.   B. The public in coastal areas.
  C. The experts on this issue.   D. Those famous people.

(　　) 3. What does the underlined word "primary" (Paragraph 3) refer to?
  A. most important   B. earliest
  C. quite natural   D. necessary

(　　) 4. We may conclude from the text that this article is a _____.
  A. foreword for a research book
  B. financial report of a certain department
  C. novel in shortened form
  D. newspaper report or magazine article

(　　) 5. What would be the best title for the text?
  A. Global Warming and Flooding
  B. Global Warming, A Serious Issue
  C. Global Warming and Agriculture
  D. Global Warning and its Effect on Economy

四、书面表达

以"My opinion on environmental protection"为题,写一篇文章,字数 80~100 字。

_____
_____
_____
_____
_____
_____

Grammar

一、从下面每小题四个选项中选出最佳选项

(　　) 1. The secretary worked all night long, _____ a long speech for the president.
　　　　A. to prepare　　　B. prepared　　　C. was preparing　　　D. preparing

(　　) 2. _____ hard and you will succeed in the exam.
　　　　A. Study　　　B. To study　　　C. Studying　　　D. Studied

(　　) 3. _____ at the door before entering, please.
　　　　A. Knock　　　B. Knocking　　　C. Knocked　　　D. To knock

(　　) 4. His parents were killed in the accident, thus _____ him an orphan.
　　　　A. leave　　　B. leaving　　　C. to leave　　　D. left

(　　) 5. _____ that he was in great danger, Eric walked deeper into the forest.
　　　　A. Not realized　　　B. Not to realize　　　C. Not realizing　　　D. Not realize

(　　) 6. Dina, _____ for months to find a job as a waitress, finally took a position at a local advertising agency.
　　　　A. struggling　　　B. struggled　　　C. having struggled　　　D. To struggle

(　　) 7. Though _____ money, his parents managed to send him to university.
　　　　A. lacked　　　B. lacking of　　　C. lacking　　　D. Lack

(　　) 8. _____ in the queue for half an hour, Tom suddenly realized that he had left his wallet at home.
　　　　A. To wait　　　B. Have waited　　　C. Having waited　　　D. Waited

(　　)9. European football is played in 80 countries, _____ it the most popular sport in the world.

　　A. make　　　B. to make　　　C. made　　　D. making

(　　)10. Finding her car stolen, _____.

　　A. a policeman was asked to help

　　B. the area was searched thoroughly

　　C. she hurried to a policeman for help

　　D. she asked to leave

(　　)11. _____ the news, they all jumped with joy.

　　A. Heard　　　B. To hear　　　C. Hear　　　D. Hearing

(　　)12. It has rained for days, _____ the river to rise.

　　A. cause　　　B. to cause　　　C. caused　　　D. causing

(　　)13. The plane crashed, _____ two of the crew and four passengers.

　　A. kill　　　B. killing　　　C. killed　　　D. to kill

(　　)14. _____ by jeep, we visited a number of cities.

　　A. Travel　　　B. Travelled　　　C. Traveling　　　D. To travel

(　　)15. Weather _____, we're going to climb mountains tomorrow.

　　A. to permit　　　B. permitted　　　C. permit　　　D. permitting

(　　)16. _____ the boy will be saved, we're very happy.

　　A. Knowing　　　B. To know　　　C. Know　　　D. Known

(　　)17. I stood there, _____ her sorting rubbish.

　　A. watch　　　B. watching　　　C. to watch　　　D. watched

(　　)18. _____ her address, we couldn't get in touch with her.

　　A. Knowing　　　B. To know　　　C. Not knowing　　　D. Not to knowing

(　　)19. They dumped waste into the river, _____ all the fish.

　　A. to kill　　　B. killed　　　C. have killed　　　D. killing

(　　)20. He walked down the hill, _____ softly to himself.

　　A. sing　　　B. to sing　　　C. sang　　　D. singing

(　　)21. _____ to the right, you will find the path.

　　A. Turning　　　B. Turned　　　C. To turn　　　D. Turn

(　　)22. _____ their teacher's voice, the students stopped talking at once.

　　A. Hear　　　B. To hear　　　C. Heard　　　D. Hearing

(　　)23. _____ how to get to the supermarket, he turned to the policeman for help.

　　A. Know　　　B. Knew　　　C. Not knowing　　　D. Known

( )24. The flood burst out in early morning, _____ many villagers.
A. To drowning   B. drown   C. drow   D. drowning

( )25. It will take you half an hour to get to the station, _____ traffic delays.
A. allow for   B. to allow for   C. allowed for   D. allowing for

( )26. She travelled widely throughout North America, _____ on environmental protection.
A. lecture   B. lecturing   C. to lecturing   D. lectured

( )27. _____ it easier to get in touch with us, you'd better keep this card at hand.
A. Made   B. Make   C. Making   D. To make

( )28. _____ over a week ago, the books are expected to arrive any time now.
A. Ordering   B. To order   C. Having ordered   D. Ordered

( )29. —I'm sorry I _____ my exercise book at home this morning.
—It doesn't matter. Don't forget _____ it here this afternoon.
A. left; to take   B. forgot; bringing   C. left; to bring   D. forgot; to bring

( )30. The cooling wind swept through out bedroom windows, _____ air conditioning unnecessary.
A. making   B. to make   C. made   D. being made

二、找出下列句子中错误的选项,并改正过来

1. I stood there, watch her sorting rubbish.
　　A　　　　B　　C　　D

2. They dumped waste into the river, kill all the fish.
　　　　A　　B　　　　　　　C　　D

3. Not know her address, we couldn't get in touch with her.
　A　　　B　　　　　　C　　　　　　　D

4. Generally speak, we need to divide daily rubbish into four categories.
　　A　　B　　　C　　　　　　D

5. The flood burst out in early morning, drown many villagers.
　　　　A　　B　　　　　　　C　　　　D

6. It will take you half an hour to get to the station, allow for traffic delays.
　　A　　　B　　　　　　C　　　　　　D

7. She travelled widely throughout North America, lecture on environmental protection.
　　　　　A　　B　　　　　　　　　　C　　　D

8. The secretary worked all night long, prepare a long speech for the president.
　　　　　A　　B　　　　　C　　　　　　　D

9. We should use recyclable packaging when shop.
　　A　　　B　　　　　C　　　　D

10. Tom went away, sing and talking happily.
　　A　　B　　C　　　　　　D

— 45 —

More Activities

一、找出与所给单词画线部分读音相同的选项

(　　) 1. consumption　A. public　　B. equipped　C. confuse　D. curious

(　　) 2. grassland　　A. climate　　B. exchange　C. gas　　　D. statement

(　　) 3. exchange　　A. exercise　B. exit　　　C. excuse　　D. example

(　　) 4. slow　　　　A. down　　　B. borrow　　C. however　D. nowadays

(　　) 5. paragraph　　A. grassland　B. exchange　C. catch　　D. water

二、汉译英

1. "绿色行动"活动_____

2. 打折的蔬菜和水果_____

3. 美食广场_____

4. 瓶装水_____

5. 自来水_____

6. 衣物交换_____

7. 全球变暖_____

8. 户外活动_____

9. 参加(活动)_____

10. 设计一张传单_____

三、用所给单词的适当形式填空

1. These events are a great way to promote environmental _____ (aware).

2. It has now become the most important _____ (globe) annual event dedicated to wildlife.

3. The North American Prairie was once one of the largest _____ (grassland) on Earth.

4. Only six of the 50 passengers _____ (survival) in the accident.

5. You can replace the tissues with _____ (handkerchief).

6. What _____ (activity) can she take part in?

7. In order to improve your health, you had better eat _____ (season) food.

8. A low-carbon lifestyle contributes a lot to environmental _____ (protect).

9. This greatly reduces electricity _____ (consume).

10. The _____ (nature) atmosphere is very good for the growth of the youth.

四、找出下列句子中错误的选项,并改正过来

1. It is no use to regret your past mistakes.
　　A　　　B　　　C　　　　　D

2. All living things work together to keep a prairie ecosystem health.
　　　A　　　　　　　B　　　　　　　　C　　　　　D

3. An ecosystem can be describe as the soil, rocks, plants, and all the processes that link these
     A   B   C   D
   things together.

4. We are looking for willed students and staff to help us go green!
        A   B   C   D

5. If Ann is interested in the clothes exchange activity, when and where should she go?
        A   B   C   D

单元检测

第一部分　英语知识运用(共分三节,满分 40 分)

第一节　语音知识:从 A、B、C、D 四个选项中找出其画线部分与所给单词画线部分读音相同的选项。(共 5 分,每小题 1 分)

(　　) 1. beneath　　A. health　　B. thus　　C. breathy　　D. smoothly

(　　) 2. process　　A. policy　　B. ecosystem　　C. confuse　　D. properly

(　　) 3. nature　　A. tableware　　B. natural　　C. capital　　D. plant

(　　) 4. develop　　A. people　　B. emission　　C. debate　　D. protect

(　　) 5. packaging　　A. hate　　B. paper　　C. transport　　D. rate

第二节　词汇与语法知识:从 A、B、C、D 四个选项中选出可以填入空白处的最佳选项。(共 25 分,每小题 1 分)

(　　) 6. The North American Prairie was once one of the largest _____ on Earth, but now only parts of it remain.
A. desserts　　B. lakes　　C. ponds　　D. grasslands

(　　) 7. An ecosystem consists of all _____, the _____ and their relationships.
A. living things; environment　　B. animals; plants
C. plants; environment　　D. animal; environment

(　　) 8. A healthy ecosystem is _____ for the _____ of all living things.
A. important; survive　　B. essential; survival
C. essential; survive　　D. importance; survive

(　　) 9. On the North American Prairie you might catch _____ of rabbits and dogs.
A. sight　　B. look　　C. see　　D. watch

(　　) 10. East _____ the mountains _____ a(n) _____ of short grass prairie.
A. from; stands; land　　B. of; lies; stretch
C. On; is; area　　D. in; is; area

( ) 11. A(n) _____ can be described _____ the soil, rocks, plants, animals, water, climate, land, and all the processes that link these things together.
A. prairie; as   B. ecosystem; of
C. ecosystem; as   D. ecosystem; to

( ) 12. The tourists felt shocked when they saw snakes _____ past their tents and hawks _____ around above their heads.
A. gliding; circling   B. circling; gliding
C. swimming; flying   D. glide; fly

( ) 13. These species might not survive in a different ecosystem—a forest or a swamp, _____.
A. like   B. such as   C. for example   D. that is to say

( ) 14. All living things are right at home here, _____ everything they need from the prairie.
A. get   B. got   C. to get   D. getting

( ) 15. Van Gogh filled his canvases with _____ sunflowers.
A. growing big yellow   B. big growing yellow
C. yellow big growing   D. growing yellow big

( ) 16. If you say that someone or something is _____, you mean they harm the environment as little as possible.
A. yellow   B. white   C. green   D. black

( ) 17. "_____" activity is on Wednesday outside Student Hall from 11 a.m. to 4 p.m. and students can exchange their used clothes then.
A. WASTE NOT   B. SWITCH OFF   C. EAT REAL   D. CLOSE NOT

( ) 18. Will you _____ the "go green" activities in our school next week?
A. join   B. take part in   C. attend   D. go

( ) 19. Thousands of _____ advertising the environmental protection activities were handed out during the festival.
A. flyers   B. notices   C. notes   D. noting

( ) 20. Almost overnight the public was drawn into a hot _____ over a person's right to die.
A. chat   B. talk   C. debate   D. fight

( ) 21. The old couple, used to country life, were _____ to move to the city to live with their son.
A. willing   B. unwilling   C. ready   D. lively

( ) 22. The rescued deer are right at home in this forest and nearly any kind of plant of the forest can be _____ of their diet.

A. member　　　B. piece　　　C. part　　　D. tight

(　　)23. John is free _____ 7 p.m. every evening _____ Monday _____ Friday.

A. since; between; and　　　B. after; from; to

C. before; since; to　　　D. in; for; to

(　　)24. Breathable, waterproof _____ is essential for most outdoor sports.

A. clothes　　　B. clothing　　　C. cloth　　　D. coat

(　　)25. If you are interested in the activity, please _____ silvia.gogreen@123123.com _____ more information.

A. connect; to　　　B. consult; with

C. contact; for　　　D. link; for

(　　)26. Low-carbon living means people try their best to _____ energy _____ and carbon _____.

A. increase; emissions; consumption　　B. reduce; consumption; emissions

C. stop; consumption; emissions　　D. go; consumption; emissions

(　　)27. A low-carbon lifestyle is a good way of _____ climate change.

A. speeding up　　B. getting rid of　　C. slowing down　　D. gain speed

(　　)28. Business investment will contribute significantly _____ economic growth.

A. to　　　B. at　　　C. on　　　D. for

(　　)29. Each of us in the society _____ the emission of _____ gases.

A. takes responsibility for; green　　B. is responsible for; greenhouse

C. take responsible for; house　　D. responsible for; house

(　　)30. The police are planning stricter measures to _____ crime.

A. combat　　　B. combine　　　C. commit　　　D. make

第三节　完形填空：阅读下面的短文，从所给的 A、B、C、D 四个选项中选出最佳的答案。(共 10 分，每小题 1 分)

Bicycle riding has many advantages. It is cheap, fun, healthy and good for the environment. If you 31 by bicycle, you don't have to buy 32 as you must when you drive cars. Besides, it costs less to repair 33 a car does. Get on a bicycle and ride around, and you may 34 something new all around you. Bicycle riding is especially 35 for health. It is a kind of good exercise. If you go to work by 36 a bicycle instead of driving a car or taking a bus, you can have a better 37 to get enough exercise you need every day. Exercise like cycling can 38 people feel better and more relaxed. It is also good for our environment. It is less noisy and does not 39 the air.

Bicycle riding is so cool. That is 40 more and more people like cycling.

( )31. A. think B. travel C. teach D. trade
( )32. A. oil B. sugar C. water D. soup
( )33. A. till B. until C. than D. unless
( )34. A. check B. cheat C. agree D. find
( )35. A. bad B. good C. thank D. sorry
( )36. A. taking B. drawing C. driving D. riding
( )37. A. chance B. change C. challenge D. control
( )38. A. hear B. see C. make D. notice
( )39. A. provide B. pollute C. produce D. protect
( )40. A. when B. where C. how D. why

第二部分 篇章与词汇理解(共分三节,满分50分)

第一节 阅读理解:阅读下列短文,从每题所给的 A、B、C、D 四个选项中选出最恰当的答案。(共30分,每小题2分)

A

Earthquakes may happen anywhere on the earth. When some plates of the earth move suddenly, an earthquake happens. Many earthquakes begin under the sea. They often happen near the mountains, too.

During an earthquake, the shaking make rocks rise suddenly and even crack(断裂) open. Houses fall, people are killed or hurt, and sometimes the whole villages or cities are destroyed.

Can we do something to keep ourselves safe from earthquakes? Scientists have studied earthquakes and made maps that show the "earthquake belts". In areas in these belts, it's possible for earthquakes to happen. In these areas we should build strong houses to fight against earthquakes.

In the future, scientists will be able to tell when and where an earthquake will be before they happen. They can also tell people what to do and how to do it.

( )41. The reason for an earthquake is _____.
　　A. some plates of the earth move suddenly
　　B. that the sea is too deep
　　C. rocks cracking open
　　D. that there are so many plates on the earth

( )42. A lot of earthquakes often happen _____.
　　A. in the area B. next to mountains
　　C. at night D. in the river

( )43. A map showing the earthquake belts will tell people _____.
　　A. what kind of houses to build

Unit 3 We Are Part of Nature

B. what kind of houses can stay up in an earthquake

C. where earthquake may happen

D. earthquakes may happen anywhere on the earth

(   )44. Which of the following is NOT true according to the passage?

A. During an earthquake people are killed or hurt.

B. The scientists can tell when and where an earthquake is now.

C. We should build strong houses to fight against earthquakes.

D. Earthquakes may happen anywhere on the earth.

(   )45. In the future, we will be no longer so afraid of earthquakes _____.

A. with the help of scientists' exact prediction

B. because of a map showing the "earthquake belts"

C. because we can guess the date and place of earthquakes

D. because there are no earthquakes

B

Different weather makes people feel different. It influences health, intelligence(智力) and feelings. In August, it is very hot and wet in the southern part of the United States. People there have heart trouble and other kinds of health problems during this month. In the northeast and the middle west, it is very hot sometimes and very cold sometimes. People in these states have more heart trouble after the weather changes in February or March.

The weather can also influence intelligence. For example, a 1983 study by scientists showed that the IQ of a group of students was very high when a very strong wind came, but after the strong wind, their IQ was 10% lower. The wind can help people have more intelligence. Very hot weather, on the other hand, can make it lower. Students in many schools of the United States often do worse on exams in the hot months of the year(July and August).

Weather also has a strong influence on people's feelings. Winter may be a bad time for thin people. They usually feel cold these months. They might feel unhappy during cold weather. But fat people may have a hard time in hot summer. At about 18℃, people become stronger.

Low air pressure(气压) may make people forgetful. People leave more bags on buses and in shops on low-pressure days. There is "good weather" for work and health. People feel best at a temperature of about 18 ℃.

Are you feeling sad, tired, forgetful, or unhappy today? It may be the weather's fault.

(   )46. _____ can have a bad effect on health.

A. Hot and wet weather   B. Good weather

C. Warm weather   D. High intelligence

(   )47. People may have more intelligence when _____ comes.

— 51 —

A. a rain B. very hot weather
C. a wind D. low air pressure

( )48. Low air pressure may make people _____.

A. forgetful B. sad C. angry D. tired

( )49. In "good weather" of 18 ℃, _____.

A. people are very forgetful B. people can't do their work well
C. thin people feel cold D. people are in better health

( )50. The article mainly tells us that _____.

A. weather influences people's health
B. weather influences people's intelligence
C. weather influences people's feelings
D. All of the above

C

Pollution inside homes and other buildings kills more than 4 million people each year. Many people die as a result of breathing smoke or from cooking over wood-powered of coal-powered stoves.

One way to reduce the number of deaths is through cooking equipment powered by the sun. Crosby Menzies, a solar power expert in a South African company, described his latest solar cooker called the "Sol-4". It is four square meters of mirrors, six to eight meters in length. It is quite a large cooker.

The "Sol-4" works by reflecting(反射) light from the sun off large mirrors. The mirrors direct (把……对准) the light at a cooking pan. Then the light heats the pan with solar energy. Within two minutes, the pan is hot enough to cook sausages and onions. In just four minutes, water can be boiled. That is as fast as cooking with natural gas or electricity.

The cooker is also much "friendlier" than other models because people do not have to stand in the sun to use it. And people can prepare meals without having to collect firewood or spend money on coal. Such individuals would be less likely to have breathing illnesses from harmful smoke.

At present, the cooker only works when the sun is shining. But engineers are working on a way to make it work without sunlight.

Each cooker costs about $2,000, which is a large amount of money for most Africans. To solve that problem, Crosby Menzies has created a non-governmental organization called Solar Cookers for Africa. It plans to raise money through donations to provide poor people with solar cooking equipment.

( )51. This passage is mainly about _____.

A. solar cooker B. smoke pollution

C. solar power experts　　　　D. breathing illnesses

(　　)52. The "Sol-4" is mainly used to _____.

　　A. shorten the time of cooking

　　B. reduce the cost of making cookers

　　C. raise money through donations to help African people

　　D. reduce the number of deaths caused by harmful smoke

(　　)53. The underlined word "individuals" most probably means "_____".

　　A. cookers　　　B. mirrors　　　C. people　　　D. experts

(　　)54. Which of the following about the "Sol-4" is TRUE?

　　A. It is six to eight square meters of mirrors.

　　B. It can work in any weather condition now.

　　C. It can also heat the pan by lighting firewood.

　　D. It is more environment-friendly than other cookers.

(　　)55. From the passage, we can infer that _____.

　　A. the "Sol-4" will be designed in a smaller size

　　B. more Africans can use the solar cookers in the future

　　C. the "Sol-4" is the first product of the South African company

　　D. the African government will provide poor people with solar cookers

第二节　词义搭配:从(B)栏中选出(A)栏单词的正确解释。(共10分,每小题1分)

(A)　　　　　　　　　　　(B)

(　　) 56. prairie　　A. a class of plants or animals whose members have the same main characteristics and are able to breed with each other

(　　) 57. species　　B. all the plants and living creatures in a particular area together considered in relation to their physical environment

(　　) 58. ecosystem　　C. a large area of flat, grassy land in North America

(　　) 59. survive　　D. an area of very wet land with wild plants growing in it

(　　) 60. swamp　　E. to continue to live or exist

(　　) 61. recyclable　　F. hold something in order to show something

(　　) 62. celebrate　　G. can be got back and reused

(　　) 63. efficient　　H. under, below something

(　　) 64. beneath　　I. change with sb for something

(　　) 65. exchange　　J. related to effect

第三节　补全对话:根据对话内容,从对话后的选项中选出能填入空白处的最佳选项。(共10分,每小题2分)

A: Hi, Mike. __66__ You can't stop coughing.

B: Oh, Steven. It's all right. I forgot to wear my pollution mask and the terrible smoke kills me.

A: ___67___ Air pollution has become a big problem here.

B: Right. Smoke and fumes from vehicles and toxic chemicals from the factories are polluting the air.

A: ___68___ Fertilisers and pesticides farmers use and human waste we produce are responsible for the pollution around us.

B: Yes. ___69___ It's time for us to take steps against pollution.

A: ___70___

B: We can fight against pollution easily and actively as long as we are aware of the importance of environment protection.

A: I agree with you. In that case, though we can't stop pollution for good, we can help lessen it effectively.

B: That's right. Combating pollution involves the combined efforts of all people on the planet.

> A. Sorry to hear that!
> B. People care so little about our environment and pollute it recklessly.
> C. Can I help you?
> D. But that's not all.
> E. So what should we do?

第三部分 语言技能应用(共分四节,满分30分)

第一节 单词拼写:根据下列句子及所给汉语注释,在答题卡上相应题号后的横线上写出该单词。(共5分,每小题1分)

71. People do their best to reduce energy _____ (消耗) and carbon emissions.

72. What he talked about was very _____ (有效的) to beginners.

73. We give a _____ (折扣) to people who use public transport.

74. We should _____ (养成) good habits in our daily life.

75. All the _____ (过程) that link these things together.

第二节 词形变换:用括号内单词的适当形式填空,将正确答案写在横线上。(共5分,每小题1分)

76. We are looking for _____ (will) students and staff to help us go green!

77. A healthy ecosystem is essential for the _____ (survive) of all living things.

78. A low-carbon lifestyle contributes a lot to _____ (environment) protection.

79. You can _____ (place) tissues with handkerchiefs.

80. Firstly, each of us is responsible for the _____ (emit) of greenhouse gases.

第三节 改错:从 A、B、C、D 四个画线处找出一处有错误的选项,并写出正确答案。(共 10 分,每小题 2 分)

81. <u>Although</u> born in a poor family, he <u>managed to</u> equip himself <u>to</u> an <u>excellent education</u>.
       A   B   C   D

82. We <u>own</u> a restaurant and <u>try to</u> be as <u>greener</u> as <u>possible</u>.
         A   B   C   D

83. All <u>live</u> things work <u>together</u> to keep a prairie <u>ecosystem</u> <u>healthy</u>.
        A   B   C   D

84. World Water Day is <u>celebrated</u> <u>around</u> the world <u>with</u> a <u>various</u> of events.
                             A   B   C   D

85. World <u>Environment</u> Day is <u>celebrated</u> <u>in</u> the 5th of June <u>every year</u>.
             A   B   C   D

81. (　　)应为_____   82. (　　)应为_____   83. (　　)应为_____
84. (　　)应为_____   85. (　　)应为_____

第四节 书面表达。(共 10 分)

保护环境人人有责。请写一篇以"环保从我做起"为主题的文章,介绍环境保护的重要性以及自己如何在生活中改变行为、践行环保措施,字数 60~80 字,首句已提供,不计入字数。

内容提示:

以前	现在(践行环保措施)
1. 坐家长的车上学	1. 走路或骑单车上学
2. 东西烂了就扔	2. 尽可能久地使用东西
3. 购物时要塑料袋	3. 购物时带自己的包
你认为作为学生应该如何做才能保护好环境?(至少两点)	

It is our duty to protect environment. After learning about environment protection in school, I have learned to make a change in my life.

_____

_____

_____

_____

_____

_____

_____

Unit 4

Beauty Is About How You Feel

Warming up

一、句型汇总

1. The lake is as beautiful as a painting. 这个湖美得像一幅画!

2. The green hills and clear water really provide an amazing view. 绿色的山峦和清澈的水构成了令人惊叹的景色。

3. This fantastic view really cheers me up. 这极美的景色真的让我心情舒畅。

4. Natural scenery can do us good. 自然风景对我们有好处。

5. We should walk into nature and enjoy its beauty whenever we have time. 我们只要有时间就应该走进自然,享受美景。

6. I visited an art gallery on Saturday. 我周六参观了一个艺术展。

7. It's too complicated for me. 对于我而言它太复杂了。

8. Enjoy it with your heart. 用心去感受它。

9. Beauty is about how you feel. 美就是你的感受。

10. Beauty is also found in many invisible things, which you can only feel with your heart and soul. 然而,美也同样存在于许多看不见的事物中,你只能用心灵去感受。

11. Music is powerful and it has the force to move the soul and change the world. 音乐是强大的,它有触动灵魂和改变世界的力量。

12. When this occurs, a sense of peace and relaxation comes over us. 这时,我们就能体会到

内心的平静和放松。

13. Love is the greatest driving force in our life. 爱是我们生活中最大的驱动力。

14. The world is filled with beauty waiting for us to appreciate. 世界充满着美,等待我们去欣赏。

15. Every time I see the faces in the classroom, my heart is filled with joy, satisfaction and happiness. 每当在教室里看到这些面孔时,我的内心都充满了快乐、满足和幸福。

二、英汉互译

1. beauty _____
2. 高兴的_____
3. shocked _____
4. 手工艺品_____
5. peaceful _____
6. 设计_____
7. comfortable _____
8. 运动之美_____
9. hopeful _____
10. 放松的_____

Listening and Speaking

一、找出与所给单词画线部分读音相同的选项

( ) 1. am<u>a</u>zing   A. h<u>a</u>ndicraft   B. f<u>a</u>ntastic   C. <u>a</u>ppreciate   D. rel<u>a</u>xation

( ) 2. c<u>o</u>mplicated   A. sh<u>o</u>cked   B. b<u>o</u>ring   C. pr<u>o</u>cess   D. zer<u>o</u>

( ) 3. br<u>ea</u>k   A. p<u>ea</u>ce   B. cr<u>ea</u>te   C. gr<u>ea</u>t   D. br<u>ea</u>th

( ) 4. p<u>ai</u>nting   A. d<u>ai</u>ry   B. pr<u>ai</u>rie   C. w<u>ai</u>tress   D. f<u>ai</u>rness

( ) 5. s<u>ou</u>l   A. disc<u>ou</u>nt   B. c<u>u</u>rious   C. greenh<u>ou</u>se   D. sh<u>ou</u>lder

二、从 B 栏中找出与 A 栏中相对应的答语

A	B
1. What do you think of the place? 2. How can I enjoy it with my heart? 3. How was your weekend? 4. Why don't you like to learn maths? 5. Do you like sports?	A. Oh, it's too complicated for me. B. Great! I visited an art gallery on Saturday. C. Of course, sports can cheer me up and make me feel relaxed. D. Oh, it really provides an amazing view! E. Well, it's hard to explain. Just follow your heart, try to appreciate it with your heart.

1. _____ 2. _____ 3. _____ 4. _____ 5. _____

三、补全对话

A: This is Jiuzhaigou.

B: Is Jiuzhaigou a nature reserve?

A: Sure. ___1___

B: Can you explain the name of it?

A: Certainly. ___2___

B: And what is the most typical scenery in Jiuzhaigou?

A: ___3___

B: ___4___

A: ___5___

B: OK, let's go!

> A. Well, it is most famous for its waterscape and virgin forests.
> B. What about the virgin forests?
> C. There are 15 nature reserves altogether in Sichuan. And it is one of them.
> D. Where shall we go first?
> E. Jiuzhaigou is named after the nine Tibetan-style villages situated in the valley.

四、场景模拟

模拟一个以参观画展为场景的对话。

Reading and Writing

一、用所给单词的适当形式填空

1. _____ (beautiful) is in the eyes of the beholder.

2. Everyone needs some free time for rest and _____ (relax).

3. The air is full of millions of _____ (visible) germs.

4. Oil painting is to be _____ (appreciate) at a distance.

5. In the _____ (silent) we could hear the clock ticking.

6. Every audience was _____ (关注的) to what he said.

7. Because of love, we _____ (团结) together.

8. Turn off the TV set in case of _____ (雷暴).

9. You are invited to _____ (探索) the beauty in our city with us.

10. I have no idea how large the _____ (物质的) universe is.

二、完形填空

Two brothers worked together on a farm. One was married and had a large __1__. The other had no wife yet. Although they lived in different houses, they shared everything they got from their farm.

One day, the single brother said to himself, "It's not __2__ that we share all the rice. I'm __3__ and I need less than my brother." So, every night he took a bag of rice from his store-room and __4__ across the field __5__ their houses, putting it into his brother's store-room.

At the same time, the married brother thought, "It's not fair to share all the rice. I'm married and I have my wife and children to __6__ me when I am __7__. However, my brother has no one to take care of his __8__." So, each night he also took a bag of rice and put it into his brother's store-room.

Several months passed by. They found __9__ strange that their rice never became less. Then, one dark night the two brothers ran into each other. Slowly they began to understand what was happening. Their bags fell onto the ground and tears __10__ their eyes at once.

( ) 1. A. group   B. family   C. class   D. team
( ) 2. A. right   B. popular   C. interesting   D. wrong
( ) 3. A. poor   B. happy   C. alone   D. rich
( ) 4. A. jumped   B. played   C. went   D. rode
( ) 5. A. from   B. through   C. off   D. between
( ) 6. A. look after   B. look for   C. look out   D. look at
( ) 7. A. worried   B. old   C. healthy   D. dead
( ) 8. A. hope   B. children   C. farm   D. future
( ) 9. A. then   B. this   C. it   D. that
( ) 10. A. appeared   B. filled   C. dropped   D. rose

三、阅读理解

Chinese painting is one of the oldest art forms in the world. Painting in the traditional style is known today in Chinese as Guohua.

Traditional Chinese painting is done with a brush dipped(浸)in black or coloured ink. Paper and silk are also needed for painting. The finished work can be put on scrolls(轴). Traditional Chinese painting includes landscape(山水)painting, figures(人物), bird and flowers. Landscape painting is regarded as the highest form of Chinese painting.

Chinese folk music is an important part of Chinese culture. It has a long history. One of the Confucianist Classics(儒家经典), *Shi Jing*, <u>contains</u> many folk songs. They are much loved by people up to now.

Traditional Chinese musical instruments are symbols of Chinese culture, such as the guqin, guzheng, pipa, erhu, xiao and chime(编钟). The sheng and suona are also popular in northern villages in China. Xi'an drum music is large traditional drum music. It is a valuable part of Chinese ancient music, and is regarded as the "living fossil(化石) of Chinese ancient music" in the world.

(　　)1. People usually use _____ for doing traditional Chinese painting.
①brushes ②ink ③colour pencils ④paper ⑤silk
A. ①②③④   B. ②③④⑤   C. ①②③⑤   D. ①②④⑤

(　　)2. The underlined word "contains" means "_____".
A. likes   B. controls   C. prevents   D. includes

(　　)3. The highest form of Chinese painting is _____.
A. landscape painting   B. figures
C. bird and flowers   D. trees

(　　)4. _____ is called the "living fossil of Chinese ancient music" in the world.
A. Folk music   B. Country music
C. Ancient music   D. Xi'an drum music

(　　)5. The passage is about _____.
A. Chinese music   B. Chinese painting
C. Chinese culture   D. Chinese history

四、书面表达

请写一篇以"美"为主题的文章,介绍美的不同种类和美的意义,字数80~100字,首句已提供,不计入字数。

内容提示:

1. 美有很多种,外在的美与内在的美、具体的美与抽象的美、大自然的美与设计的美等;

2. 寻找美的事物能帮助我们发现生活的真谛,也能让我们变成更好的自己;

3. 举例说明你生活中一件美的事物;

4. 只要有心,美处处都在。

Beauty

There are many kinds of beauty.

_____
_____
_____
_____
_____
_____

Grammar

一、从下面每小题四个选项中选出最佳选项

( )1. _____ your umbrella, or you'll catch a cold on such a rainy day.
  A. Take   B. To take   C. Taking   D. Taken

( )2. Tom, _____ carefully! There's a school ahead.
  A. driving   B. drive   C. drives   D. to drive

( )3. Sally, _____ the window, please.
  A. doesn't open   B. opens   C. don't open   D. not open

( )4. _____, please! Let's begin our lesson.
  A. Be quiet   B. Be noisy   C. Don't be quiet   D. Noisy

( )5. —Jack, don't always copy what others do. _____ your head, please.
  —Thanks for telling me.
  A. Using   B. Used   C. Uses   D. Use

( )6. Don't drink coffee before going to bed, or you _____ easily.
  A. don't fall asleep   B. won't fall asleep
  C. didn't fall asleep   D. haven't fallen asleep

( )7. —As we all know, life is short but amazing.
  —_____ it, and you will find the pleasure of life.
  A. Enjoy   B. To enjoy   C. Enjoying   D. Enjoyed

(   )8. —Don't take pictures here, please.
      —_____.
      A. No way   B. Sorry, I won't   C. Here you are   D. It's a pleasure

(   )9. Let's go sightseeing tomorrow, _____?
      A. will you   B. shall we   C. do you   D. do we

(   )10. _____ great fun it is to have ice cream in hot summer!
      A. What a   B. How   C. What   D. How a

(   )11. _____ funny the 3D movie is! I really enjoy it.
      A. How   B. What   C. What a   D. How a

(   )12. _____ cheap furniture!
      A. What   B. What a   C. How   D. What an

(   )13. _____ cheap the furniture is!
      A. What   B. What a   C. How   D. What an

(   )14. _____ useful information it is!
      A. What an   B. How   C. What   D. How a

(   )15. _____ useful dictionary it is!
      A. What a   B. How   C. What   D. How a

(   )16. —Jane won the first prize in the English speech contest.
      —_____ big progress she has made! She used to be weak in English.
      A. How   B. How a   C. What   D. What a

(   )17. _____ time flies!
      A. What   B. How   C. How quick   D. What quick

(   )18. _____ beautiful dress! Whose is it?
      A. How   B. What   C. What a   D. How a

(   )19. _____ bright sunshine! Let's have a picnic.
      A. How   B. What   C. What a   D. How a

(   )20. Study hard, _____ you will pass the final exam.
      A. or   B. and   C. yet   D. but

(   )21. The boy wanted to ride his bike in the street, but his mother told him _____.
      A. not to   B. not to do   C. not do it   D. do not to

(   )22. Unless _____ to speak, you should remain silent at the conference.
      A. invited   B. inviting   C. being invited   D. having invited

(   )23. —Do you mind my taking this seat?
      —_____
      A. Yes, sit down   B. No, of course not

C. Yes,take it please D. No,you can't take it

(　　)24. _____ the road,don't forget to look both ways.

A. As crossing B. While you cross

C. While crossing D. Cross

(　　)25. Of all the things in the world,I think life and love are _____.

A. very much precious B. more than precious

C. the preciousest D. the most precious

(　　)26. The workers did all _____ good care of the old man.

A. they could to take B. they could take

C. which they could to take D. what they could to take

(　　)27. What surprised me was not what he said but _____ he said it.

A. the way B. in the way

C. in the way which D. in the way that

(　　)28. —Is that a book on farming? If so,I want to borrow _____.

—Yes,it is.

A. this B. it C. one D. the one

(　　)29. —Are you a volunteer now?

—No,but I _____. I worked for the City Sports Meeting last year.

A. used to B. used to be C. used to do D. was used to

(　　)30. —You should have thanked her before you left.

—I meant _____ but when I was leaving I couldn't find her anywhere.

A. to thank B. to C. / D. thanking

二、句型转换

1. He works hard at his lessons! （改为感叹句）

_____ he works at his lessons!

2. The teacher was very shocked when she heard the news. （改为感叹句）

_____ the teacher was when she heard the news!

3. We are facing a very complicated problem. （改为感叹句）

_____ a _____ problem we are facing.

4. The painting of landscape is very beautiful. （改为感叹句）

_____ a painting of landscape _____ !

5. You'd better not smoke here. （改为祈使句）

_____!

6. You should check your homework before you hand it in. (改为祈使句)
   _____.

7. You should not play in the street. It is dangerous. (改为祈使句)
   _____.

8. If it is necessary, we will finish it ahead of time. (改为省略句)
   _____.

9. Give me your name and address, please. (改为省略句)
   _____.

10. It is well done. (改为省略句)
    _____.

More Activities

一、找出与所给单词画线部分读音相同的选项

( ) 1. l<u>i</u>ghtning   A. <u>u</u>nite   B. l<u>i</u>quid   C. f<u>u</u>rniture   D. exh<u>i</u>bition

( ) 2. compli<u>c</u>ated   A. sho<u>ck</u>ed   B. deligh<u>t</u>ed   C. ama<u>z</u>ed   D. mov<u>ed</u>

( ) 3. <u>ex</u>plore   A. <u>ex</u>hibition B. <u>ex</u>plain   C. <u>ex</u>tra   D. <u>ex</u>ample

( ) 4. cl<u>a</u>ssical   A. cl<u>a</u>ss   B. l<u>a</u>ne   C. fl<u>a</u>sh   D. fr<u>a</u>me

( ) 5. <u>th</u>understorm   A. <u>th</u>irsty   B. whe<u>th</u>er   C. smoo<u>th</u>   D. wi<u>th</u>out

二、英汉互译

1. cheer me up _____   2. 心灵_____

3. do us good _____   4. 驱动力_____

5. follow one's heart _____ 6. 自然风景_____

7. a flash of lightning _____ 8. 古典音乐_____

9. the rising sun _____   10. 手工制作的家具_____

11. liquid eyes _____   12. 平静下来_____

三、用所给单词的适当形式填空

1. The speed and engine's sound are also _____(好极了) to me.

2. I prefer listening to Chinese _____(古典的) music.

3. He was able to put _____(复杂的) thoughts into simple words.

4. They are endowed with _____ (艺术的) talents.

5. The lake is as beautiful as a _____ (画).

6. Sometimes even a simple act of _____ (kind) can change a person's life.

7. The media has a _____ (power) influence on public opinion.

8. Every time I see the faces of the kids, my heart is filled with _____ (satisfy) and happiness.

9. The green hill and clear water really provide an _____ (amaze) view.

10. She was _____ (delight) at the result.

四、找出下列句子中错误的选项,并改正过来

1. Even the <u>most simple</u> sound in life can be <u>the most</u> <u>beautiful</u> "music".
     A B   C   D

2. When in <u>motion</u>, <u>the</u> racing car <u>is</u> <u>filled</u> <u>of</u> energy.
       A B   C D

3. The <u>faces</u> of my students are young and <u>thirst</u> <u>for</u> <u>knowledge</u>.
     A   B C D

4. Sometimes the <u>merely</u> <u>slight</u> of good food <u>makes</u> <u>me</u> happy.
          A   B   C D

5. There is <u>no</u> <u>lacking</u> of <u>beauty</u> in life, but our eyes don't <u>always</u> see it.
      A B   C   D

单元检测

第一部分　英语知识运用(共分三节,满分40分)

第一节　语音知识:从A、B、C、D四个选项中找出其画线部分与所给单词画线部分读音相同的选项。(共5分,每小题1分)

(　　) 1. rela<u>x</u>ation A. n<u>a</u>tural   B. h<u>a</u>ndicraft C. <u>a</u>ttentive D. fr<u>a</u>me

(　　) 2. <u>u</u>nite   A. th<u>u</u>nderstorm B. s<u>u</u>nshine C. conf<u>u</u>se   D. l<u>u</u>xury

(　　) 3. <u>ar</u>tistic A. w<u>ar</u>m   B. h<u>ar</u>m   C. popul<u>ar</u> D. lun<u>ar</u>

(　　) 4. phys<u>i</u>cal A. exc<u>i</u>ting B. chance   C. appreciate D. artistic

(　　) 5. po<u>w</u>er A. follo<u>w</u>   B. kno<u>w</u>ledge C. kno<u>w</u>   D. co<u>w</u>

第二节　词汇与语法知识:从A、B、C、D四个选项中选出可以填入空白处的最佳选项。(共25分,每小题1分)

(　　) 6. He seems in low spirits today, how can we _____ him _____?
    A. give; up   B. cheer; up   C. bring; up   D. pick; up

(　　)7. Your bag is twice as _____ as mine.
　　A. expensive　　　　　　　　B. more expensive
　　C. most expensive　　　　　　D. the most expensive

(　　)8. I am so tired. Sleep might do me _____ right now.
　　A. well　　B. better　　C. good　　D. a good

(　　)9. _____ we met with difficulties, they came to help us.
　　A. However　　B. Whenever　　C. Whatever　　D. Wherever

(　　)10. _____ down! Don't get so excited.
　　A. Sit　　B. Put　　C. Slow　　D. Calm

(　　)11. The speaker likes to have _____ audience.
　　A. attentive　　B. creative　　C. attractive　　D. native

(　　)12. Your life will always _____ challenges.
　　A. is full of　　B. be filled of　　C. be full with　　D. be filled with

(　　)13. Would you be kind enough to _____ to my house for a chat tomorrow?
　　A. look over　　B. come over　　C. go over　　D. take over

(　　)14. If you have any trouble, I'm _____ to help.
　　A. looking　　B. willing　　C. seeing　　D. looking forward

(　　)15. The woman dressed in blue is _____ mother.
　　A. Mary and Alice
　　B. Mary's and Alice's
　　C. Mary and Alice's
　　D. Mary's and Alice

(　　)16. _____ I think of you, I feel a sense of comfort.
　　A. Any time　　B. Every time　　C. All time　　D. Some time

(　　)17. The issue is _____ complicated _____ I can't deal with it.
　　A. such; that　　B. so; as to　　C. so; that　　D. too; to

(　　)18. Chinese paper-cutting shows us the beauty of _____.
　　A. nature　　B. design　　C. painting　　D. handicraft

(　　)19. —The boys are not doing a good job at all, are they?
　　—_____.
　　A. I guess not so
　　B. I don't guess
　　C. I don't guess so
　　D. I guess not

(　　)20. _____ from Beijing to London!
　　A. How long way it is
　　B. How long way is it
　　C. What a long way it is
　　D. What a long way is it

(　　)21. Oh, Tom, _____ you gave us!

Unit 4 Beauty Is About How You Feel

A. how a pleasant surprise B. how pleasant surprise
C. what a pleasant surprise D. what pleasant surprise

(   )22. _____ fantastic time the children had playing hide-and-seek int the park!
A. How   B. What   C. How a   D. What a

(   )23. _____ example he set for us!
A. How good   B. What good   C. What a good   D. How a good

(   )24. _____ at my door before you enter my room, please.
A. Knocking   B. Knocked   C. To knock   D. Knock

(   )25. —Sorry for being late for the party.
—_____ earlier next time, will you?
A. Coming   B. To come   C. Having come   D. Come

(   )26. "_____ that again!" Father shouted to me when I was found playing with fire.
A. Never to do   B. Never do   C. Do never   D. Don't never do

(   )27. _____ in bed. It's bad for your eyes.
A. Not to read   B. Don't read   C. Don't to read   D. Not read

(   )28. If you want to stay, let me know, _____?
A. will you   B. shall we   C. do you   D. do we

(   )29. —We can invite Nick and Nora to Shanghai Disneyland with us.
—_____? I will give them a call right now.
A. What for   B. Why not   C. Why   D. What

(   )30. —I was wondering if we could go skiing on the weekend.
—_____ good.
A. Sound   B. Sounded   C. Sounds   D. Sounding

第三节 完形填空:阅读下面的短文,从所给的 A、B、C、D 四个选项中选出最佳的答案。(共 10 分,每小题 1 分)

If you have never watched the sun rise up in the morning, then you really should do so. It is good for your spirit. You need to go out early when the __31__ is still dark and full of stars. Then find a comfortable place to stand or sit in. The black sky slowly begins to __32__ into a dark blue while the stars are getting to disappear. Then as the __33__ of the sky begins to become lighter, and then red, pink and purple clouds slowly appear. Just as you enjoy the __34__, the sky changes again. It becomes orange, then yellow and you must be __35__ as the sun slowly climbs over the sea level. At the same time, the sun makes the world bright __36__ we can see everything. And the sun makes the birds __37__. Some sing with joy and others fly to the sky. When you watch __38__, the morning light wind kisses your face and makes the leaves dance and the trees wave. Take your time to watch the sun rise up. Keep it __39__ in your heart forever. Be a sunrise as well. Send your light when you laugh and sing. __40__ your light when you help others. Share your light with the world. Then you will live the happy life you expect.

( )31. A. street   B. light   C. house   D. sky
( )32. A. put   B. through   C. turn   D. cut
( )33. A. size   B. shape   C. color   D. smell
( )34. A. beauty   B. meal   C. party   D. book
( )35. A. talented   B. excited   C. worried   D. tired
( )36. A. so that   B. in order to   C. even if   D. as soon as
( )37. A. get lost   B. fly away   C. wake up   D. hang out
( )38. A. us   B. her   C. them   D. him
( )39. A. waiting   B. singing   C. walking   D. shining
( )40. A. Make   B. Spread   C. Keep   D. Hide

第二部分　篇章与词汇理解(共分三节,满分50分)

第一节　阅读理解:阅读下列短文,从每题所给的 A、B、C、D 四个选项中选出最恰当的答案。(共30分,每小题2分)

A

A farmer has four lambs(羔羊). One is black, and the other three are white. The black lamb is kind to the white lambs. But the white lambs don't want to make friends with him. They think he is ugly. The farmer always gives bad food to the black lamb.

One winter day, the four lambs go out to eat grass. They go far away from home. Suddenly, it begins to snow. It is such a heavy snow that the ground is all white soon. They get lost.

When the farmer finds that his lambs are not home, he goes out to look for them. There is snow everywhere. Suddenly, he sees something black. He goes to it. Oh, it is his black lamb! And the white lambs are there, too. The farmer says happily, "Thanks to the black lamb, I can find you!"

( )41. What do the white lambs think of the black lamb?
　　A. Great   B. Kind   C. Ugly   D. Beautiful
( )42. The underlined word "them" in Paragraph 3 refers to(指代) _____.
　　A. the white lambs
　　B. the black lamb and the three white lambs
　　C. the black lambs
　　D. the black lamb and the four white lambs

(   )43. The lambs can't find the way home because _____.

　　A. they are far away from home　　B. there is snow everywhere

　　C. it is too cold(冷) outside　　D. they don't want to go back home

(   )44. The farmer finds all the lambs after _____.

　　A. he sees the black lamb　　B. he sees the white lambs

　　C. he hears the sound of the lambs　　D. they come back home

(   )45. What can we learn from the story?

　　A. The early bird catches the worm(虫子).

　　B. A friend in need is a friend indeed.

　　C. Appearance(外貌) is important in our life.

　　D. Don't tell a person by his appearance.

B

What can you do with your spilled(溢出) drink? Just clean it, right? But Italian artist Giulia can turn it into works of art.

One day, Giulia spilled her coffee all over the table. Seeing this, she got a good idea. She used the spoon(匙) as a pen and then drew with coffee. After practicing a lot, she got better and better at it. Her amazing coffee art becomes really welcome online now.

After seeing these beautiful works, more and more people, become interested in coffee art.

When she draws with coffee, Giulia gets her ideas from many different things, like famous artworks, buildings and the human bodies. She uses everything around her to create(创作) art. Today, Giulia is one of the world's best coffee artists.

(   )46. Where does Giulia come from?

　　A. America　　B. England　　C. Italy　　D. Canada

(   )47. What does the underlined word "it" in Paragraph 2 refer to?

　　A. Selling coffee　　B. Making coffee

　　C. Drinking coffee　　D. Drawing with coffee

(   )48. Which of the following can be Giulia's artwork with coffee?

A.　　B.　　C.　　D.

(   )49. What is Giulia now?

　　A. One of the world's best coffee artists.

　　B. One of the world's best coffee teachers.

C. One of the world's best coffee makers.

D. One of the world's best coffee farmers.

(   )50. What can we know from the passage?

A. Giulia spilled her coffee on her book one day.

B. More and more people become interested in coffee art.

C. Giulia can only use spilled coffee to create art.

D. Giulia was angry (生气的) when her coffee spilled.

C

When I was growing up in America, I was ashamed of my mother's Chinese English. Because of her English, she was often treated unfairly. People in department stores, at banks, and at restaurants did not take her seriously, did not give her good service, pretended not to understand her, or even acted as if they did not hear her.

My mother has realized the limitations of her English as well. When I was fifteen, she used to have me call people on phone to pretend I was her. I was forced to ask for information or even to yell at people who had been rude to her. One time I had to call her stockbroker (股票经纪人). I said in an adolescent (青少年的) voice that was not very convincing, "This is Mrs. Tan." And my mother was standing beside me whispering loudly, "Why he don't send me check, already two weeks late."

And then, in perfect English I said: "I'm getting rather anxious. You agreed to send the check two weeks ago, but it hasn't arrived." Then she talked more loudly. "What does he want? I will come to New York and say it in front of his boss." And so I turned to the stockbroker again, "I can't tolerate any more excuses. If I don't receive the check immediately, I am going to have to speak to your manager when I am in New York next week."

The next week we ended up in New York. While I was sitting there red-faced, my mother, the real Mrs. Tan, was shouting to his boss in her broken English. When I was a teenager, my mother's broken English embarrassed me. But now, I see it differently. To me, my mother's English is perfectly clear, perfectly natural. It is my mother tongue. Her language, as I hear it, is vivid, direct, and full of observation and wisdom. It was the language that helped shape the way I saw things, expressed ideas, and made sense of the world.

(   )51. Why was the author's mother poorly served?

A. She was unable to speak good English.

B. She was often misunderstood.

C. She was not clearly heard.

D. She was not very polite.

(   )52. From Paragraph 2, we know that the author was _____.

Unit 4　Beauty Is About How You Feel

　　　　A. good at pretending　　　　　　B. rude to the stockbroker

　　　　C. ready to help her mother　　　　D. unwilling to phone for her mother

(　　)53. After the author made the phone call, _____.

　　　　A. they forgave the stockbroker

　　　　B. they failed to get the check

　　　　C. they went to New York immediately

　　　　D. they spoke to their boss at once

(　　)54. What does the author think of her mother's English now?

　　　　A. It confuses her.　　　　　　　B. It embarrasses her.

　　　　C. It helps her understand the world.　　D. It helps her tolerate rude people.

(　　)55. We can infer from the passage that Chinese English _____.

　　　　A. is clear and natural to non-native speakers

　　　　B. is vivid and direct to non-native speakers

　　　　C. has a very bad reputation in America

　　　　D. may bring inconvenience(不便) in America

第二节　词义搭配:从(B)栏中选出(A)栏单词的正确解释。(共10分,每小题1分)

　　　　　(A)　　　　　　　　　　　　　　(B)

(　　)56. explore　　　　　　A. connected with material things

(　　)57. relaxation　　　　　B. greatly pleased

(　　)58. attentive　　　　　C. difficult to analyze or understand

(　　)59. invisible　　　　　D. examine minutely

(　　)60. appreciate　　　　E. listening or watching carefully with interest

(　　)61. artistic　　　　　　F. a storm with thunder and lightning and a lot of heavy rain

(　　)62. complicated　　　　G. impossible or nearly impossible to see

(　　)63. delighted　　　　　H. to recognise the good qualities of sb. /sth.

(　　)64. thunderstorm　　　I. a feeling of an absence of tension or worry

(　　)65. physical　　　　　J. connected with art or artist

第三节　补全对话:根据对话内容,从对话后的选项中选出能填入空白处的最佳选项。(共10分,每小题2分)

A:It is very nice of you to invite me.

B:＿66＿ Will you take a seat at the head of the table. It's an informal dinner, please don't stand on ceremony. Mr Liu, would you like to have some chicken?

A:Thank you. This is my first time to come to a Chinese restaurant.

B：Generally speaking,Cantonese food is light;Shanghai food is rather oily;and Hunan dish is very spicy,having a strong and hot taste.

A：Chinese dishes are exquisitely prepared,delicious,and very palatable. __68__

B：Mr Liu,could you care for another helping?

A：__69__

B：Did you enjoy the meal?

A：__70__ It's such a rich dinner.

B：I'm so glad you like it.

A：Thank you very much for your hospitality.

> A. It's the most delicious dinner I've had for a long time.
> B. They are very good in color,flavour and taste.
> C. I am very glad you could come,Mr Liu.
> D. No more,thank you. I'm quite full.
> E. Could you tell me the different features of Chinese food?

第三部分　语言技能应用(共分四节,满分 30 分)

第一节　单词拼写：根据下列句子及所给汉语注释,在横线上写出该单词。(共 5 分,每小题 1 分)

71. The fog is so thick that we are _____ (看不见的).

72. You can go and _____ (欣赏)Western paintings.

73. She sells _____ (手工艺品)to the tourists.

74. We need to buy some new _____ (家具)for our new house.

75. Science and technology make it possible for scientists to _____ (探索)the universe.

第二节　词形变换：用括号内单词的适当形式填空,将正确答案写在横线上。(共 5 分,每小题 1 分)

76. Diet and _____ (relax)are two important keys to good health.

77. These are _____ (physics) changes while those are chemical changes.

78. They were _____ (shock)at the news.

79. When you look at a painting,don't consider its _____ (artist)value.

80. Kunming is a city with a lot of _____ (nature)scenery.

第三节　改错：从 A、B、C、D 四个画线处找出一处错误的选项,并写出正确答案。(共 10 分,每小题 2 分)

81. Doing more physical exercise do us good.
　　　A　　　　　B　　　　C　D

82. However, beautiful is also found in many invisible things.
    　　A　　　　B　　　　　C　　　　　D

83. What interesting role she played in the movie!
    　　A　　　B　　　C　　D

84. Let's take a walk outside, will we?
    　　A　　　B　　　　　　C　D

85. The world is filled with beauty wait for us to appreciate it.
    　　　　　　A　　B　　　C　　D

81.(　　)应为_____ 82.(　　)应为_____ 83.(　　)应为_____

84.(　　)应为_____ 85.(　　)应为_____

第四节　书面表达。(共10分)

生活中并不缺少美,而是缺少发现美的眼睛。只要我们用心感受就能发现身边的美好,它可能是一个人、一桩事、一件物品、一处风景……也会给我们的生活增添光彩。请根据自己的经历或见闻,以"Life is Full of Beauty"为题,分享你在生活中发现的美及感受。

要求:

1. 讲述一件事情。

2. 表达真情实感。

3. 字数80~100字。

Life is Full of Beauty

Unit 5

It's Necessary to Develop Soft Skills

Warming up

一、句型汇总

1. It is a great honour to participate in the project. 很荣幸能参加这个项目。

2. Planning and working smarter are the best solutions when we have a busy schedule. 当我们工作安排比较忙时,更高明地做好计划与工作才是最佳解决方法。

3. I like taking on challenges and learning how to become an efficient member of the team. 我乐于接受挑战并学习在团队中如何成为一名高效的成员。

4. It is also necessary to have team spirit in our group. 在我们团队中团队精神也是必要的。

5. When you're searching for a job, it is useful to know how to describe your skills. 找工作时,知道如何描述自己的技能很有用。

6. Soft skills refer to non-technical interpersonal and intrapersonal abilities that help you improve job performance and cooperate better with other people. 软技能是非技术性的人际交往能力和自我管理能力,它可以帮助你提升工作表现,更好地与他人合作。

7. In general, the most desired soft skills are communication skills, team spirit and problem-solving skills. 总体而言,最需要具备的软技能是沟通能力、团队精神以及解决问题的能力。

8. Communication is what allows you to build bridges between you and co-workers, express your needs and persuade others to accept your ideas. 沟通能帮助你与同事建立纽带，让你可以表达自己的需求，说服他人接受你的观点。

9. This means you understand and believe that ideas, plans, decisions and actions will be better carried out when you cooperate with others. 这意味着你理解并且相信与他人合作才能更好地实现想法、实施计划、执行决定并付诸行动。

10. You should be able to solve problems in creative ways. 你应该能够创造性地解决问题。

11. Both hard skills and soft skills need to be learnt and developed, if you want to achieve success in your career. 如果你希望在职业生涯获得成功，那么这两种技能都应学习与培养。

二、英汉互译

1. challenge _____   2. 自信 _____
3. solution _____   4. 沟通技能 _____
5. time management _____   6 积极的态度 _____
7. problem-solving skill _____   8. 合作 _____
9. impressive _____   10. 参加 _____

Listening and Speaking

一、找出与所给单词画线部分读音相同的选项

(   ) 1. co<u>u</u>rage   A. f<u>ou</u>nd   B. tr<u>ou</u>ble   C. d<u>a</u>ngerous   D. gr<u>ou</u>p

(   ) 2. solu<u>tion</u>   A. exhibi<u>tion</u>   B. ques<u>tion</u>   C. sugges<u>tion</u>   D. diges<u>tion</u>

(   ) 3. <u>u</u>niverse   A. s<u>u</u>rroundings   B. d<u>u</u>stbin   C. <u>a</u>ttitude   D. sol<u>u</u>tion

(   ) 4. <u>c</u>onfidence   A. <u>c</u>ompete   B. solution   C. <u>c</u>omplaint   D. <u>c</u>omplicated

(   ) 5. <u>s</u>pirit   A. <u>i</u>mpressive   B. del<u>i</u>ght   C. organ<u>i</u>se   D. cl<u>i</u>mate

二、从 B 栏中找出与 A 栏中相对应的答语

A

1. I usually organise and prioritise my tasks.
2. We are glad that you've joined us.
3. I'm tired of calling you guys again and again.
4. What have you learnt from your last job?
5. Good afternoon, may I help you?

B

A. I have learnt to be patient when dealing with customers' complains and try my best to solve them.
B. I haven't received my package yet.
C. Very impressive!
D. I'm sorry for the trouble.
E. It is a great honour to participate in the project.

1. _____ 2. _____ 3. _____ 4. _____ 5. _____

三、补全对话

A：Good morning, sir. How are you today?

B：Fine, thank you. 1

A：Mr. Diego Lopez?

B：Yes, that's right.

A：You're staying with us for two nights.

B：Yes, that's correct.

A：I'm sorry, Mr. Lopez. 2 Normally our check-in is from 2 pm.

B：Yes, I know that, but my flight arrived early.

A：I'm sorry but housekeeping are still cleaning your room.

B：That's not very good. 3

A：Well, you're welcome to store your luggage with us. May I suggest you have a cup of coffee in the restaurant? 4

B：OK, but how long will that be?

A： 5

B：Thank you. I'd appreciate it.

A. When your room's ready, I'll come and get you. Is that OK?
B. I have a reservation(预定) in the name of Lopez.
C. I'll ask housekeeping to do your room as quickly as possible.
D. Your room isn't quite ready yet.
E. What do you suggest me do?

四、场景模拟

模拟快递员 A 和 Mr. Brown 之间的对话，Mr. Brow 由于工作很忙，没有时间接收包裹，和快递员约定明天下午再次送包裹。

_____
_____
_____
_____
_____

Reading and Writing

一、用所给单词的适当形式填空

1. We offer free _____ (technique) support.

2. Humor is very important in _____ (personal) relationships.

3. Money is a _____ (necessary) of life, but not all of life.

4. The _____ (compete) for job is fierce.

5. He gets along very well with his _____ (同事) in the company.

6. We can't _____ (竞争) with them on price.

7. It's the soft _____ (技能) that often get you the job.

8. They tried in vain to _____ (说服) her to go.

9. We are _____ (面临) with a difficult choice.

10. Hope to _____ (合作) with you and look forward to serving you.

二、完形填空

Cindy and Anna were best friends. Some days they could spend hours happily together without any argument, but other days they just could not __1__ on what to do.

One day they decided to play in the garden near their school. "Come on, let's play chess," Anna said.

"I don't want to play chess," Cindy replied.

"We always do what you want to do, Cindy. It's my turn to make a __2__," Anna said. She was getting a little unhappy and __3__, leaving Cindy alone.

Cindy was very angry. __4__ she got home, she found she still had Anna's notebook in her schoolbag. "Well, I'm not giving it back to her today. I'm too mad at her," Cindy thought.

The next day at school, their teacher Mrs. Stone __5__ their notebooks. But Anna didn't have hers, and she looked __6__. Cindy knew she should tell Mrs. Stone that she had the notebook, but she was __7__ mad at Anna.

When it was time for lunch, Cindy finally told Mrs. Stone the __8__. "Thank you for being __9__, Cindy. I'm sure Anna will be thankful that you have given me her notebook," said Mrs. Stone.

Later, Mrs. Stone asked the two girls together and talked with them. Mrs. Stone helped them __10__ that it was a good idea to take turns to decide the activity. They became best friends again.

( ) 1. A. agree   B. live   C. depend   D. try

( ) 2. A. promise   B. project   C. decision   D. dialogue

( ) 3. A. went over   B. went on   C. went by   D. went away

( ) 4. A. Because   B. After   C. Unless   D. If

( ) 5. A. gave away   B. asked for   C. handed in   D. paid for

( ) 6. A. worried   B. normal   C. proud   D. relaxed

( ) 7. A. still   B. never   C. usually   D. almost

( ) 8. A. chance   B. method   C. truth   D. rule

( ) 9. A. patient   B. honest   C. active   D. quiet

( ) 10. A. describe   B. explain   C. guess   D. realize

三、阅读理解

Working on a team is a good thing. But it can bring you some troubles. If people on your team are not good at communicating, you may often feel terrible. To create a successful team, good communication is the most necessary part for both team members and the leader. The following are some helpful suggestions.

* Don't criticize other people. When someone on your team does something wrong, don't criticize him. You can help him to find out reasons and then help him to solve the problem. Criticizing your team members too often may make them keep away from you. As a result, you may feel lonely.

* Think about other people's ideas carefully. When someone tells you about his ideas, you should think about them carefully, no matter how silly they may seem. This shows you are interested in his ideas and makes him feel good.

* Listen to other people actively. When someone is speaking to you, you need to listen

Unit 5 It's Necessary to Develop Soft Skills

to him actively. If you're unclear about something, you should ask him about it. By doing this you can clear up any confusion(困惑) before moving on.

∗ Share your ideas with other people. When you have a new idea, talk about it with your team members. This helps to improve the idea. Besides this, it also helps to improve your relationships between you and your team members.

(　　)1. For team members and the leader, _____ is the most necessary part to create a successful team.
   A. communicating well   B. dealing with criticism
   C. sharing ideas   D. listening to others

(　　)2. If you criticize your team members too often, they will _____.
   A. feel lonely   B. keep away from you
   C. be afraid of you   D. correct their mistakes

(　　)3. If Lisa tells you about her idea, but you think her idea is foolish, you should _____.
   A. get angry and criticize her
   B. think about her idea carefully
   C. explain to her why her idea is silly
   D. forget her silly idea and laugh at her

(　　)4. The best title of the passage may be "_____".
   A. Criticize Others or Not   B. Share Ideas with Others
   C. Learn to Listen to Others   D. Work Well on a Team

(　　)5. How many suggestions are mentioned in the passage?
   A. One   B. Two   C. Three   D. Four

四、书面表达

请你为新华中学设计一个招聘英语老师的广告。

_____
_____
_____
_____
_____

Grammar

一、从下面每小题四个选项中选出最佳选项

( ) 1. To improve your spoken English you should practise _____ it every day.
    A. speak   B. to be spoken   C. speaking   D. to speak

( ) 2. The classroom needs _____.
    A. cleaned   B. clean   C. cleaning   D. to clean

( ) 3. On hearing the joke, they couldn't help _____.
    A. laughed   B. laughing   C. to laugh   D. being laughed

( ) 4. They left the office without _____ a word.
    A. having said   B. saying   C. to say   D. said

( ) 5. I don't mind _____ by bus, but I hate _____ in queues.
    A. to travel; standing   B. traveled; standing
    C. traveling; to stand   D. traveling; standing

( ) 6. We suggested _____ in hotels but the children were anxious _____ out.
    A. sleeping; to camp   B. sleeping; camping
    C. to sleep; to camp   D. to sleep; camping

( ) 7. —I must apologize for _____ ahead of time.
    —That's all right.
    A. letting you not know   B. not letting you know
    C. letting you know not   D. letting not you know

( ) 8. She is not used _____ in the city.
    A. to live   B. to living   C. to have lived   D. live

( ) 9. I really appreciate _____ to relax with you on this nice island.
    A. to have had time   B. having time
    C. to have time   D. to having time

( ) 10. She didn't remember _____ him before.
    A. having met   B. have met   C. to meet   D. to having met

( ) 11. Have you forgotten _____ $1,000 from me last month? Will you please remember _____ it tomorrow?
    A. to borrow, to bring   B. borrowing, bringing

Unit 5 It's Necessary to Develop Soft Skills

C. to borrow, bringing   D. borrowing, to bring

(   )12. —You were brave enough to raise objections at the meeting.
—Well, now I regret _____ that.
A. to do   B. to be doing   C. to have done   D. having done

(   )13. We regret _____ you that we are unable to offer you the job.
A. told   B. to tell   C. telling   D. tell

(   )14. Though it sounds a bit expensive, it is worth _____.
A. being bought   B. buying   C. to buy   D. buying it

(   )15. I apologise for _____ my promise.
A. having not kept   B. not having kept
C. not to have kept   D. have not to keep

(   )16. We are both looking forward to _____ next week.
A. going on vocation   B. go on vocation
C. be going on vocation   D. have gone on vocation

(   )17. He devoted his life to _____ super hybrid rice(杂交水稻).
A. study   B. be studied   C. studying   D. have studied

(   )18. Seeing is _____.
A. to believe   B. believing   C. believed   D. to believing

(   )19. He admitted _____ the money.
A. to take   B. taking   C. took   D. take

(   )20. He was busy _____ for the test.
A. having prepared   B. prepare
C. to prepare   D. preparing

(   )21. I don't feel like _____ to see the film.
A. go   B. gone   C. to go   D. going

(   )22. It is no good _____ in the exam.
A. to cheat   B. cheating   C. having cheated   D. cheat

(   )23. It is a waste of time _____ computer games.
A. play   B. to play   C. playing   D. played

(   )24. I found it useless _____ with him.
A. arguing   B. argueing   C. to argue   D. argue

(   )25. These days he is considering _____ his job.
A. to change   B. changed   C. been changed   D. changing

(   )26. —Can I smoke here?

—Sorry, we don't allow _____ here.
A. people smoking   B. people smoke
C. to smoke   D. smoking

( )27. _____ a language requires time and efforts.
A. Learning   B. learn   C. To learn   D. Learnt

( )28. His parents insist on _____ to college.
A. him to go   B. he should go   C. he go   D. his going

( )29. You can't imagine what difficult we had _____ home in the snowstorm.
A. walked   B. walk   C. to walk   D. walking

( )30. Tony was very unhappy for _____ to the party.
A. having not been invited   B. not having invited
C. having not invited   D. not having been invited

二、找出下列句子中错误的选项，并改正过来

1. He never complained about work overtime.
     A   B C D

2. No paying attention to small mistakes will make big ones.
 A B   C   D

3. I prefer staying at home to go out on such a rainy day.
    A   B C D

4. We don't allow such thing happening again.
  A B C   D

5. The boy took away the woman's watch without seeing.
   A   B   C   D

6. Be laughed at in public made him angry.
 A B   C D

7. Those officers narrowly escaped been killed in the battle.
   A   B   C   D

8. Having not enough money prevented him from entering the university.
 A   B   C D

9. I know who is responsible for break the window.
    A   B   C

10. Watch too much TV does harm to your eyes.
  A   B C D

Unit 5 It's Necessary to Develop Soft Skills

More Activities

一、找出与所给单词画线部分读音相同的选项

(   ) 1. ti<u>r</u>ed   A. disappointe<u>d</u>   B. fac<u>ed</u>   C. solv<u>ed</u>   D. check<u>ed</u>

(   ) 2. c<u>a</u>reer   A. c<u>r</u>eative   B. w<u>o</u>rkplace   C. s<u>o</u>ciety   D. f<u>a</u>ced

(   ) 3. g<u>r</u>aph   A. m<u>a</u>nager   B. l<u>a</u>st   C. <u>a</u>ttitude   D. h<u>a</u>ndle

(   ) 4. inte<u>r</u>personal A. pe<u>r</u>suade   B. cle<u>r</u>k   C. inte<u>r</u>nship D. inse<u>r</u>t

(   ) 5. p<u>a</u>rticipate   A. c<u>o</u>llar   B. st<u>a</u>ndard   C. qu<u>a</u>rter   D. <u>a</u>rgue

二、英汉互译

1. creative thinking _____   2. 团队精神_____

3. interpersonal skills _____   4. 工作表现_____

5. workplace etiquette _____   6. 职业规划_____

7. management skills _____   8. 解决问题的能力_____

9. positive attitude _____   10. 沟通技能_____

三、用所给单词的适当形式填空

1. College students are supposed to make their career _____(规划) in advance.

2. Everyone should take a _____(积极的) attitude towards life.

3. _____(人际交往) skills can help you cooperate better with other people.

4. Team _____(精神) is necessary not only for a team's success but also for personal development.

5. They lack basic _____(communicate) skills in dealing with interpersonal issues.

6. He made a public apology for the team's bad _____(perform).

7. The problem was _____(solve) successfully.

8. Time _____(manage) is the greatest challenge for me in high school.

9. In modern society, the students who have _____(create) thinking are needed most.

10. The government needs a _____(practice) solution.

四、找出下列句子中错误的选项,并改正过来

1. When you're <u>searching for</u> a job, it is <u>useful</u> <u>to know</u> how <u>describe</u> your skills.
   　　　　　　　A　　　　　　　　B　　　　C　　　　　　D

— 83 —

2. Once, a customer came in, <u>demanded</u> we <u>repair</u> the appliance he <u>had</u> <u>bought</u>.
          A   B   C D

3. The customer <u>told</u> us he <u>has</u> <u>paid</u> by <u>credit card</u>.
      A   B C   D

4. I found a <u>payment</u> that <u>looked</u> right, <u>giving</u> the information <u>provided</u> by the customer.
     A   B   C   D

5. You should try <u>to forget</u> the <u>terrible</u> experience, and <u>go on</u> <u>to</u> your life.
       A   B   C D

单元检测

第一部分　英语知识运用(共分三节,满分 40 分)

第一节　语音知识:从 A、B、C、D 四个选项中找出其画线部分与所给单词画线部分读音相同的选项。(共 5 分,每小题 1 分)

( )1. techni<u>que</u> A. <u>ch</u>eck B. ex<u>ch</u>ange C. <u>Ch</u>ristmas D. <u>ch</u>allenge

( )2. r<u>e</u>fer A. p<u>e</u>rformance B. p<u>e</u>rsuade C. d<u>e</u>liver D. pr<u>e</u>fer

( )3. t<u>ea</u>m A. gr<u>ea</u>t B. m<u>ea</u>nt C. m<u>ea</u>n D. cr<u>ea</u>tive

( )4. s<u>ear</u>ch A. h<u>ear</u>t B. l<u>ear</u>nt C. h<u>ear</u> D. w<u>ear</u>

( )5. d<u>e</u>lay A. r<u>e</u>cipe B. d<u>e</u>mand C. comp<u>e</u>te D. sch<u>e</u>dule

第二节　词汇与语法知识:从 A、B、C、D 四个选项中选出可以填入空白处的最佳选项。(共 25 分,每小题 1 分)

( )6. I am tired of _____ your guys again and again.
   A. to call B. calling C. have called D. being called

( )7. Hard skills involve _____ with equipment, data, software and other tools.
   A. working B. to work C. be working D. being working

( )8. Soft skills _____ non-technical interpersonal and intrapersonal abilities.
   A. belong to B. refer to C. see to D. take to

( )9. In _____, the most desired soft skills are communication skills, team spirit and problem-solving skills.
   A. generally B. common C. generous D. general

( )10. I like _____ challenges and learning how to become an efficient member of the team.
   A. taking after B. taking place C. taking in D. taking on

( )11. Both hard skills and soft skills need _____ and _____.

Unit 5 It's Necessary to Develop Soft Skills

  A. to learn, develop   B. to be learnt, developed
  C. learning, developing   D. both B and C

(　　)12. Besides, you will also _____ challenges.
  A. be facing with   B. are facing   C. face with   D. be faced with

(　　)13. I am trying to persuade him _____ the plan.
  A. to give up   B. giving up   C. to be given up   D. gave up

(　　)14. This decision can be better _____ when you cooperate with others.
  A. broken out   B. put out   C. carried out   D. turned out

(　　)15. I always try my best to get over the difficulties I'm faced with. We can replace the underlined phrase with _____.
  A. overcome   B. come over   C. go over   D. take over

(　　)16. My employees are willing _____ me.
  A. follow   B. to following   C. to follow   D. followed

(　　)17. You should _____ solve problems in creative ways.
  A. be able   B. can   C. able   D. be able to

(　　)18. What do you think is the _____ of life?
  A. personality   B. nature   C. character   D. spirit

(　　)19. I hope you can win this game. Don't _____ me _____.
  A. knock; down   B. broke; down   C. put; down   D. let; down

(　　)20. No one can avoid _____ by advertisements.
  A. to be influenced   B. being influenced
  C. influencing   D. having influenced

(　　)21. I can't imagine _____ in the entrance examination, for she has never been to school.
  A. she succeeding   B. her succeeding
  C. she succeed   D. her to succeed

(　　)22. My radio isn't working. It needs _____.
  A. to repair   B. repairing   C. to repairing   D. be repaired

(　　)23. I delayed _____ your letter because I had been away for a week.
  A. to post   B. posting   C. to be posted   D. post

(　　)24. After finishing his homework, he went on _____ a letter to his parents.
  A. writing   B. to write   C. wrote   D. written

(　　)25. —What do you think of the book?
  —Oh, excellent. It's worth _____ a second time.

    A. to read   B. to be read   C. reading   D. being read

( )26. _____ hard can result in failure.

    A. Not working   B. No working   C. Not work   D. Don't work

( )27. _____ is easier than doing.

    A. To talk   B. Talking   C. Talk   D. Talked

( )28. Grandma had a lot of trouble _____ your handwriting.

    A. to read   B. to see   C. reading   D. in seeing

( )29. He was afraid _____ for being late.

    A. of seeing   B. of being seen   C. to be seen   D. to have seen

( )30. Would you mind _____ quiet for a moment? I'm trying _____ a form.

    A. keeping, filling out   B. to keep, to fill out

    C. keeping, to fill out   D. to keep, filling out

第三节　完形填空：阅读下面的短文，从所给的 A、B、C、D 四个选项中选出最佳的答案。(共 10 分，每小题 1 分)

  Living skills are not just about survival(生存) skills, such as washing and cooking. They refer to different kinds of active skills. They can help us deal with the __31__ of everyday life. In fact, we teenagers usually can't __32__ all kinds of problems in life only by the knowledge learned in school. We need to use living skills to change our knowledge __33__ social abilities.

  There are many living skills for us to learn. Among all the skills, social skills are considered as the most important, __34__ we must learn how to communicate with others and get on well with others in our daily life.

  Besides, the skills of relieving pressure(缓解压力) are also important. In the __35__ society, people get too much pressure from others and even themselves. They may cause __36__, anger and even illness. Then it's important for us to __37__ how to relax ourselves in a proper way.

  Living skills are very __38__ for our future development. They can improve our self-confidence, responsibility and independence, and they can help us form good __39__ as well. Once we have these skills, we can face the problem __40__. In a word, if we want to lead a happy life or succeed in study, we must improve ourselves in such living skills.

( )31. A. choices   B. questions   C. problems   D. discoveries

( )32. A. believe in   B. talk about   C. look for   D. get over

( )33. A. for   B. from   C. with   D. into

( )34. A. so   B. and   C. all   D. but

( )35. A. special   B. modern   C. safe   D. polite

( )36. A. pity   B. fun   C. fear   D. silence

( )37. A. wonder   B. find   C. know   D. tell
( )38. A. cheap   B. necessary   C. worth   D. clear
( )39. A. ways   B. results   C. signs   D. habits
( )40. A. easily   B. slowly   C. widely   D. quickly

第二部分　篇章与词汇理解(共分三节,满分50分)

第一节　阅读理解:阅读下列短文,从每题所给的A、B、C、D四个选项中选出最恰当的答案。(共30分,每小题2分)

A

It is important to have good human relationships. Good human relationships mean that you get well with the people around you. Most people say that they like you. Very few people or even nobody says that they do not want to be friends with you.

What helps to build good human relationships? Personality(人格)comes first of all. If you are open, warm and helpful, people will like you a lot. They welcome such personality.

Being humorous(幽默) also helps you to have good human relationships among people. Jokes help to make people laugh. Laughing is good for health. A famous Chinese saying goes: If you laugh once, you will be ten years younger. If you enjoy playing jokes on others and your jokes make them unhappy, they will not like you.

Good health helps to build good relationships, too. People always like to stay or work with a healthy person. If you are often sick, that means you can't always work together with others. So it is really important to exercise often to stay healthy.

( )41. This passage is all about _____.
　　A. good human relationships   B. good health
　　C. good personality   D. playing jokes on others

( )42. What does the underlined phrase "human relationships" mean in Chinese?
　　A. 身体状况   B. 知足常乐   C. 风趣幽默   D. 人际关系

( )43. If a person is open, warm and helpful, then this person _____.
　　A. is friendly   B. has a bad mood
　　C. doesn't have too many friends   D. talks a lot about himself

( )44. Is it right to play jokes on other people to make them feel bad?
　　A. Yes, it is right.   B. No, it isn't right.
　　C. It's not very wrong.   D. The text doesn't answer this question.

( )45. How many ways does the text tell us to build good human relationships?
　　A. Only one   B. Two   C. Three   D. More than three

B

Bob and Jackie joined a company together just after finishing high school. They both worked very hard. After several years, the boss made Jackie sales manager but Bob a salesman. One day Bob could not take it anymore. He handed in his resignation letter(辞职信) to the boss and complained that the boss did not value hard-working workers.

The boss knew that Bob didn't work hard for the company all these years, but in order to help Bob to realize the difference between him and Jackie, the boss asked Bob to do the following. "Go and find out if there is anyone selling watermelons in the market." Bob went, returned and only said, "Yes." The boss asked, "How much per kilogram?" Bob went back to the market to ask and returned to answer, " $ 12 per kilogram."

The boss told Bob to ask Jackie the same question. Jackie went, returned and said, "Boss, only one person selling watermelons. $ 12 per kilogram, 100 for 10 kilograms. He has 340 melons in all. On the table are 58 melons, and every melon weighs about 7 kilograms, bought from the South two days ago. They are fresh and red."

Bob realized the difference between himself and Jackie. He decided not to leave but to learn from Jackie.

My dear friends, you know, a more successful person is more careful, thinks more and understands in depth. For the same matter, he sees several years ahead, while you see only tomorrow. The difference between a year and a day is 365 times, so how could you win?

Think: how far have you seen ahead in your life?

(　　)46. Why did Bob hand in his resignation letter?

  A. Because he worked very hard.

  B. Because he just finished high school.

  C. Because he was made a sale manager.

  D. Because he was still a salesman after years.

(　　)47. What did the boss ask Bob to go to the market for?

  A. To learn to sell watermelons in the market later.

  B. To know the people who sell watermelons well.

  C. To let Bob realize the difference between him and Jackie.

  D. To help Bob learn the way to be a very successful person.

(　　)48. How much will be paid for 10 kilograms of watermelons?

  A. 100.　　　B. 120.　　　C. 150.　　　D. 340.

(　　)49. Which of the following statements is TRUE?

  A. The boss wanted to sell watermelons.

B. Bob was valued by the boss very much.

C. Jackie was more careful and think more than Bob.

D. The boss thought Bob worked hard for the company.

(　　)50. What did Bob decide to do at last?

　　A. To leave the company.　　B. To learn from Jackie.

　　C. To look for a new job.　　D. To go back to school.

C

A famous foreign company in China wanted a clerk for its public relation department.

A beautiful girl with a master's degree went through a lot of challenges and her name was on the list. In the final stage she faced an interview together with another girl. Both of them were outstanding, not only in looks but also in education.

The girl was successful in the interview. It seemed that she would get the chance. At last the examiner asked her,"Can you come to the office next Monday?"Shocked by unexpected question, the beautiful girl couldn't make a decision at the moment. So she said,"I have to talk with my parents before I give an answer."The examiner felt surprised but said calmly."If so, let's wait till you are ready."

The next day, the girl came to tell the examiner that her parents had agreed to let her begin work next Monday. But the examiner said regretfully"Sorry, another suitable candidate has got the job. You had better try another place."The beautiful girl was surprised. She asked for an explanation and was told,"What is needed here is a person who knows her own mind."

That was how a good opportunity <u>right under the nose</u> of a beautiful girl ran away.

(　　)51. The beautiful girl wanted to ask her parents for advice because _____.

　　A. she didn't like the job

　　B. she didn't expect the examiner would ask such a question

　　C. she didn't want to answer the question

　　D. her parents would be angry if she didn't ask them

(　　)52. We can learn from the passage that _____.

　　A. the company lost its best clerk

　　B. no girl got the job

　　C. the other girl who failed at the last interview might got the job

　　D. the examiner was very pleased with the girl

(　　)53. The examiner regarded _____ as the most important.

　　A. a person's confident　　B. a person's knowledge

　　C. a person's age　　D. a person's beautiful looks

( )54. The underlined phrase "right under the nose of" probably means _____.
A. 就在鼻子下 B. 想要得到的 C. 没有把握的 D. 就在眼前

( )55. The best title for the passage above might be _____.
A. Make Decision With Your Parents
B. A Successful Interview
C. Use Your Own Mind
D. Answer the Examiner's Question Quickly

第二节 词义搭配:从(B)栏中选出(A)栏单词的正确解释。(共10分,每小题1分)

(A)   (B)

( )56. impressive   A. relating to technique
( )57. let down   B. making a strong or vivid impression or producing a strong effect
( )58. technical   C. engage in a contest or measure oneself against others
( )59. interpersonal   D. make sb. adopt a certain position, belief, or course of action
( )60. persuade   E. occurring among or involving several people
( )61. solution   F. concerned with actual use or practice
( )62. practical   G. the method for solving a problem
( )63. schedule   H. work together on a common enterprise of project
( )64. compete   I. fail to meet the hopes or expectations of
( )65. cooperate with   J. an ordered list of times at which things are planned to occur

第三节 补全对话:根据对话内容,从对话后的选项中选出能填入空白处的最佳选项。(共10分,每小题2分)

A：Tell me a little bit about yourself.

B： __66__

A：What kind of personality do you think you have?

B： __67__

A：What would you say are your weaknesses and strengths?

B：Well, I'm afraid I'm a poor speaker, however I'm fully aware of this, so I've been studying how to speak in public. I suppose my strengths are I'm persistent(坚持不懈的) and a fast-learner.

A：Do you have any licenses or certificates?

B： __68__

A：How do you get along with others?

B： __69__

A：Ok, now if you have any questions, please feel free to ask me.

— 90 —

Unit 5 It's Necessary to Develop Soft Skills

B：No, I have none, thanks!

A：Thank you for your interest in our company.

A：Thank you, sir. Goodbye.　__70__

A. I have a driver's license, and I am a CPA (Certified Public Accountant).

B. I'm very co-operative and have good teamwork spirit.

C. My name is Mike and I live in Singapore. I was born in 1980. My major was electrical engineering.

D. Well, I approach things very enthusiastically(热情地), I think, and I don't like to leave things half-done. I'm very organized and extremely capable.

E. Thank you for your time.

第三部分　语言技能应用(共分四节,满分30分)

第一节　单词拼写：根据下列句子及所给汉语注释,在横线上写出该单词的正确形式。(共5分,每小题1分)

71. They refused to _____ (合作) with an American company.

72. A clerk must know how to _____ (对付) difficult customers.

73. The musician has perfect _____ (技术) but little expression.

74. The president has a tight _____ (日程安排) today.

75. I was completely _____ (失望的) to hear that.

第二节　词形变换：用括号内单词的适当形式填空,将正确答案写在横线上。(共5分,每小题1分)

76. Your progress in Chinese is very _____ (impress).

77. There's no simple _____ (solve) to this problem.

78. It is also _____ (necessity) to have team spirit in our group.

79. Teaching young children is a _____ (challenge) and rewarding job.

80. Who won the _____ (compete)?

第三节　改错：从A、B、C、D四个画线处找出一处错误的选项,并写出正确答案。(共10分,每小题2分)

81. It is a great honour to participate the project.
　　　A　　B　　C　　　　D

82. However, hard skills and soft skills are never meant competing with each other.
　　A　　　　　　　　　　　B　　　C　　D

83. Communication is what allows you building bridges between you and co-workers.
　　　　A　　　　B　　C　　D

—— 91 ——

84. It is no use to cry over the spilt milk.
        A   B   C   D

85. Not finish her homework made her upset.
    A   B   C   D

81.(　)应为_____　　82.(　)应为_____　　83.(　)应为_____

84.(　)应为_____　　85.(　)应为_____

第四节　书面表达。(共 10 分)

请写一篇以"Soft Skills"为主题的文章,介绍软技能的重要性和如何培养软能力,字数 80~100 字,首句已提供,不计入字数。

内容提示:

1. 软技能是当今社会人才必备的重要能力,它包括了人际交往能力与自我管理能力,如沟通能力、团队合作能力以及组织工作能力等。

2. 不同于硬技能,软技能更多的是体现人们创造性地解决问题的能力。

3. 举例说明自己拥有的一个软技能以及它的作用。

4. 软技能需要我们不断学习与训练。只要坚持,一定能拥有它。

Soft Skills

Soft skills are necessary to us nowadays.

_____

_____

_____

_____

_____

Unit 6

It's like a Home Away from Home

Warming up

一、句型汇总

1. It's like a home away from home. 它就像是家之外的另一个家。

2. Health experts have warned that smoking can lead to heart disease, lung cancer and other health problems. 健康专家提醒吸烟可能导致心脏病、肺癌和其他健康问题。

3. Second-hand smoking is also terrible. 吸二手烟也很糟糕。

4. How about "Smokeless Success"? "戒烟即成功"怎么样？

5. They will succeed to some degree if they give up smoking. 从某种程度上说，如果他们戒烟了，他们就成功了。

6. People who live in the same area meet and help each other at the centre. 住在同一片区域的人们在中心里见面并相互帮助。

7. They join groups to share their experience with other members and seek advice if they have problems. 他们加入不同的团体与其他成员分享经验，并在遇到问题时寻求他人的建议。

8. Can the groups get people out of trouble? 这些团体能帮人们摆脱困境吗？

9. They are helpful in a lot of ways. 他们在很多方面都很有帮助。

10. It is wonderful to always work in a group of some sort. 总是能在某一团体中工作是很棒

的(一件事)。

11. The best way to reward people for their help is to pass on their kindness. 报答他人的帮助最好的方法就是传递他们的善意。

12. Fragrance always lingers in the hand that gives the rose. 赠人玫瑰,手留余香。

13. Community service is performed by an individual or a group of people for the benefit of the public or an organisation. 社区服务是由个人或群众出于公共利益或组织利益而提供的。

14. Serving a community allows us to build stronger connections with other people living in the same area. 服务社区让我们与生活在同一区域的其他人建立起更密切的联系。

15. This sense of belonging is as important as what we get from our own family. 这种归属感和我们从家庭中获得的(归属感)一样重要。

16. It feels great to be needed and relied on. 被需要和被依赖的感觉是很棒的。

17. Participating in community service is an easy and convenient way to pass on love. 参与社区服务是一种简单、方便的传递爱的方式。

18. We should work together to make our community warmer and better. 我们要共同努力,使我们的社区变得更温暖、更美好。

19. We've got the whole world in our hands. 世界尽在我们手中掌握。

20. I came across this programme,"Your Neighbourhood Flea Market"at the community centre. 在社区中心,我偶然发现了"社区跳蚤市场"活动。

21. I volunteered, and was responsible for promoting the programme. 我自愿参加,并且负责宣传项目。

22. I signed up for a programme,"Teaching Seniors to Use Smartphones". 我报名参加了一项活动——"教老年人使用智能手机"。

23. Teaching the elderly might be the most meaningful work I have ever done. 教老年人可能是我做过的最有意义的工作了。

二、英汉互译

1. community service _____   2. 筹钱_____
3. donate clothes _____   4. 好处,受益_____
5. organise _____   6. 报名_____
7. succeed _____   8. 归属感_____
9. rely on _____   10. 偶遇_____
11. decorate _____   12. 脱离困境_____

Unit 6 It's like a Home Away from Home

Listening and Speaking

一、找出与所给单词画线部分读音相同的选项

( ) 1. b<u>e</u>nefit   A. b<u>e</u>lief   B. d<u>e</u>mand   C. d<u>e</u>corate   D. d<u>e</u>sign

( ) 2. c<u>a</u>ncer   A. c<u>a</u>mpaign   B. l<u>a</u>ne   C. <u>a</u>ttentive   D. cl<u>i</u>mate

( ) 3. t<u>ai</u>lor   A. c<u>a</u>ptain   B. g<u>ai</u>n   C. c<u>er</u>tain   D. <u>ai</u>rport

( ) 4. tr<u>ou</u>ble   A. th<u>ou</u>ght   B. en<u>ou</u>gh   C. pr<u>ou</u>d   D. sh<u>ou</u>t

( ) 5. su<u>cc</u>ess   A. a<u>cc</u>ording   B. a<u>cc</u>ount   C. a<u>cc</u>ident   D. a<u>cc</u>omplish

二、从 B 栏中找出与 A 栏中相对应的答语

A

1. Do they go there very often?
2. What do they do to help each other?
3. Smoking is bad for health.
4. Have you got a name for the campaign?
5. What are they doing there?

B

A. I agree, second-hand smoking is also terrible.
B. Err, how about "Smokeless Success"?
C. Yes, they spend time there regularly.
D. They are carrying out a fire drill.
E. They join groups to share experience and seek advice.

1. _____ 2. _____ 3. _____ 4. _____ 5. _____

三、补全下面对话

A: Hi, Bob. Where are you heading?

B: 1

A: Oh, why do you go there? It's for the old people.

B: 2

A: A volunteer?   3

B: 4

A: What else?

B: And, last week I signed up a programme "Teaching Seniors to Use Smartphone".

A: Sounds great.   5

— 95 —

B: Welcome!

> A. I want to become a volunteer, too.
> B. I talk with the old people, play chess, do some cleaning…
> C. I'm a volunteer in the Senior Citizen's club.
> D. What do you do there?
> E. I'm going to the Senior Citizen's club.

四、场景模拟

编写一组相约参与社区植树活动的对话。

提示词汇:this weekend/Tree Planting Day/the People's Park/the green life style/meaningful

_____
_____
_____
_____
_____
_____

Reading and Writing

一、用所给单词的适当形式填空

1. I did such things as _____ (decorate) the flea market.

2. He was seen _____ (enter) the building.

3. I was very happy when I saw my neighbors _____ (exchange) items.

4. _____ (serve) the needs of future generations is what we have to think about now.

5. It is great to be _____ (need).

6. Community service is the best way _____ (pass) on love.

7. You'd better _____ (seek) advice from your parents.

8. Everyone should realise the _____ (important) of learning.

9. People _____ (live) in same areas meet at the community.

10. They spent much time _____ (volunteer) for this work.

二、完形填空

Each nation has many volunteers who help to take care of others. They __1__ books to the people in hospitals or homes for the aged. Sometimes they just visit them and play games with them or listen to their __2__. Other young volunteers go and work in the homes of people who are sick or __3__. They paint, clean up, __4__ their houses or do their shopping.

For boys who no longer have __5__, there is an organization called Big Brothers. College students and other men take these boys to baseball games or fishing places and help them to get to know things that boys __6__ learn from their fathers.

Each city has a number of clubs __7__ boys and girls can go to play games or learn crafts(工艺). Some of these clubs organize short trips to the mountains, beaches, or other places of interest __8__. Most of these clubs use high school and college students as volunteers because they are young enough to __9__ the names of boys and girls.

Volunteers believes that the happiest people in the world are those who help to __10__ happiness to others.

( )1. A. sell   B. read   C. throw   D. show
( )2. A. voices   B. speeches   C. songs   D. problems
( )3. A. young   B. happy   C. old   D. hungry
( )4. A. pollute   B. repair   C. build   D. remove
( )5. A. brothers   B. sisters   C. fathers   D. mothers
( )6. A. usually   B. never   C. only   D. seldom
( )7. A. which   B. who   C. when   D. where
( )8. A. nearby   B. faraway   C. abroad   D. home
( )9. A. report   B. forget   C. remember   D. choose
( )10. A. cause   B. bring   C. take   D. lend

三、阅读理解

阅读下面短文,从每题所给的 A、B、C、D 四个选项中选出最佳答案。

Community service is an important component(组成部分) of education here at our university. We encourage all students to volunteer for at least one community activity before they graduate. A new community program called "One On One" helps elementary students who've fallen behind. Your education majors might be especially interested in it because it offers the opportunity to do some teaching, that is, tutoring in math and English. You'd have to volunteer two hours a week for one semester(学期). You can choose to help a child with math, English, or both. Half-hour lessons are fine, so you could do a half hour of each subject two days a week.

Professor Dodge will act as a mentor(导师) to the tutors—he'll be available to help you with lesson plans or to offer suggestions for activities. He has office hours every Tuesday and Thursday afternoon. You can sign up for the program with him and begin the tutoring next week.

I'm sure you'll enjoy this community service… and you'll gain valuable experience at the same time. It looks good on your resume, too, showing that you've had experience with children and that you care about your community. If you'd like to sign up, or if you have any questions, stop by Professor Dodge's office this week.

(　　)1. What is the purpose of the talk?

  A. To explain a new requirement for graduation.

  B. To interest students in a new community program.

  C. To discuss the problems of elementary school students.

  D. To recruit(招募) elementary school teachers for a special program.

(　　)2. What is the purpose of the program that the speaker describes?

  A. To find jobs for graduating students.

  B. To help education majors prepare for final exams.

  C. To offer tutorials to elementary school students.

  D. To provide funding for a community service project.

(　　)3. What does Professor Dodge do?

  A. He advises students to participate in the special program.

  B. He teaches part-time in an elementary school.

  C. He observes elementary school students in the classroom.

  D. He helps students prepare their resumes.

(　　)4. What should students interested in the tutorials do?

  A. Contact the elementary school.

  B. Sign up for a special class.

  C. Submit(建议) a resume to the mentor.

  D. Talk to Professor Dodge.

(　　)5. Whom do you think the speaker talks to?

  A. Teachers.　　　B. Parents.　　　C. Residents.　　　D. Students.

四、书面表达

假设你将成为一名社区志愿者,简述你在志愿服务时可能遇到的情况:

Unit 6 It's like a Home Away from Home

To Be a Community Volunteer,字数 80~100 字.

_____
_____
_____
_____
_____
_____

Grammar

一、从下面每小题四个选项中选出最佳选项

1. Fragrance always lingers in the hand _____ gives the rose.
   A. where   B. that   C. whom   D. whose

2. We visited the factory _____ makes computers.
   A. where   B. in which   C. which   D. it

3. Our teacher, _____ was an Englishman, was a good doctor.
   A. that   B. who   C. which   D. whom

4. I will never forget the day _____ I spent with you.
   A. that   B. in which   C. when   D. where

5. Is this factory _____ we visited last year?
   A. where   B. which   C. the one   D. at which

6. He is a tailor _____ job is to make clothes.
   A. whose   B. that   C. whom   D. who

7. The girl _____ gives me a needle and thread was my sister.
   A. which   B. that   C. whom   D. whose

8. She hasn't got enough money _____ she can buy the rings.
   A. which   B. that   C. with which   D. for which

9. Is there anything _____ I can do for you?
   A. which   B. who   C. that   D. what

10. I've read all the books _____ were borrowed from the library.
    A. where   B. /   C. which   D. that

11. I have a friend _____ has a good camera.
    A. who   B. whom   C. whose   D. he

12. The man _____ today left this message for you.
    A. called   B. has called   C. whom called   D. who called

13. The man _____ is our new teacher.
    A. whom you spoke   B. whom you spoke to
    C. you spoke   D. you spoke with whom

14. I don't think the number of the people _____ this happens is very large.
    A. whom   B. who   C. of whom   D. to whom

15. Do you work near the building _____ color is yellow?
    A. that   B. which   C. whose   D. its

16. Here is the girl _____ school bag has been stolen.
    A. who   B. whom   C. whose   D. her

17. The number of people _____ lost homes reached as many as 250,000.
    A. who   B. whom   C. whose   D. which

18. It sounded like a train _____ was going under my house.
    A. it   B. which   C. /   D. whom

19. The car _____ my uncle had just bought was destroyed in the earthquake.
    A. which   B. whom   C. who   D. whose

20. The boy _____ we saw yesterday was John's brother.
    A. which   B. who   C. whose   D. what

21. The swimmer _____ you are asking about is over there.
    A. whom   B. which   C. whose   D. what

22. The building _____ window are bright at night is our school building.
    A. which   B. that   C. whom   D. whose

23. Is the river _____ through that town very large?
    A. which flows B. flows   C. that flowing   D. whose flows

24. The games in _____ the young men competed were difficult.
    A. whom   B. whose   C. which   D. that

25. He helped his father on the small town _____ they lived.
    A. which   B. that   C. when   D. where

26. I can tell you _____ he told me last week.
    A. all which   B. all what   C. all   D. all who

27. I like the way _____ he talks and laughs.

A. which　　　　B. to which　　　　C. in which　　　　D. what

28. She likes to use words _____ is clear to him.
　　A. of which the meaning　　　　B. which the meaning
　　C. whose of meaning　　　　　　D. the meaning of which

29. I'm one of the boys _____ never late for school.
　　A. that is　　　B. who is　　　C. who are　　　D. who was

30. He is the most charming speaker _____ I have ever heard.
　　A. who　　　　B. that　　　　C. whose　　　　D. which

二、找出下列句子中错误的选项,并改正过来

1. These who have plenty of money will help their friend.
   　A　　B　　C　　　　　　　　　　D

2. This is the longest train which I have ever seen.
   　　　　A　　B　　　　C　　　D

3. Which we all know, swimming is a very good sport.
   　A　　　B　　　　　C　　　　　　　D

4. I'll never forget those years which I lived on the farm which you visited last week.
   　　　　　　　A　　　B　　　　C　　　　　　D

5. The radio which I bought it last week has gone wrong.
   　　　　　A　　　　B　　　　　　C　　　D

6. Mr. Herpin is one of the foreign experts who is working in China.
   　　　　　　　　　　　　　　　A　　B　C　　　　D

7. They talked for about an hour of things and persons who they remembered in the school.
   　　　　　A　　B　　　　　C　　　　　　　　D

8. My glasses, with which I was like a blind man, fell to the ground.
   　　　　A　　B　　C　　　　　　　　　　D

9. He is a man of great experience, from who much can be learned.
   　　　　　A　　B　　　　　　　C　　D

10. I have bought the same dress which she is wearing.
    　　A　　　　　B　　　　C　　　D

More Activities

一、找出与所给单词画线部分读音相同的选项

(　　)1. pr<u>o</u>perty　　A. <u>a</u>wesome　　B. c<u>o</u>mmerce　　C. p<u>o</u>sition　　D. c<u>o</u>mmunicate

(　　)2. thr<u>ow</u>　　　A. wind<u>ow</u>　　B. p<u>ow</u>erful　　C. all<u>ow</u>　　　D. fl<u>ow</u>er

(　　)3. rel<u>y</u>　　　　A. bic<u>y</u>cle　　B. st<u>y</u>le　　　　C. w<u>o</u>rry　　　D. l<u>o</u>nely

(　　)4. li<u>ng</u>er A. lu<u>n</u>ch B. da<u>ng</u>erous C. stro<u>ng</u>er D. stra<u>n</u>ge

(　　)5. <u>n</u>eighbour A. <u>n</u>either B. <u>r</u>eign C. h<u>ei</u>ght D. <u>s</u>eize

二、英汉互译

1. 社区服务_____

2. come across _____

3. 传递爱_____

4. care for public property _____

5. 网上冲浪_____

6. teaching assistant _____

7. 对……有好处/害处_____

8. as important as _____

9. 征求意见_____

10. participate in _____

11. 设计海报_____

12. sense of belonging _____

三、用所给单词的适当形式填空

1. They like to see their students get _____ (involve) in the community.

2. I taught older people there how _____ (text) with smartphone.

3. It made me _____ (feel) good to help others.

4. _____ (teach) the elderly might be the most meaningful work.

5. This kind of things was _____ (tire), but I was very happy.

6. The programme items has built strong _____ (connect) among people.

7. I felt that troubles had _____ (strong) the relations between us.

8. Community service is benefit for the public and an _____ (organise).

9. Everyone should realise the _____ (important) of community service.

10. It's really bad for them. I hope they will become _____ (health).

四、找出下列句子中错误的选项,并改正过来

1. I <u>must</u> be <u>responsible</u> <u>in</u> <u>promoting</u> the programme.
  A   B   C D

2. It feels great <u>to</u> be <u>need</u> by people <u>who</u> are <u>in</u> need.
     A B   C D

3. The book <u>which</u> Mo Yan <u>writes</u> <u>it</u> is very <u>famous</u>.
    A   B C   D

4. He <u>likes</u> the <u>books</u> <u>which</u> <u>written</u> by Mo Yan.
  A   B   C D

5. The man <u>stood</u> at the tree <u>was</u> my <u>favorite</u> teacher.
   A B   C   D

Unit 6　It's like a Home Away from Home

单元检测

第一部分　英语知识运用(共分三节,满分40分)

第一节　语音知识:从 A、B、C、D 四个选项中找出画线部分与所给单词画线部分读音相同的选项。(共 5 分,每小题 1 分)

(　　)1. participate　　A. popular　　B. career　　C. cartoon　　D. quarter

(　　)2. passion　　A. language　　B. danger　　C. courage　　D. nation

(　　)3. wonderful　　A. develop　　B. province　　C. social　　D. honey

(　　)4. impression　　A. decision　　B. television　　C. passion　　D. occasion

(　　)5. performed　　A. worked　　B. educated　　C. fetched　　D. climbed

第二节　词汇与语法知识:从 A、B、C、D 四个选项中选出可以填入空白处的最佳选项。(共 25 分,每小题 1 分)

(　　)6. You deserve a _____ for being so helpful.
　　A. reward　　　　B. regard　　　　C. toward　　　　D. worthy

(　　)7. _____ bad you feel, keep trying.
　　A. No matter when　　　　　　B. No matter what
　　C. No matter how　　　　　　D. No matter which

(　　)8. As parents we have a responsibility to give our children a sense of _____.
　　A. longing　　　B. beloving　　　C. belonging　　　D. belong

(　　)9. We organised a campaign _____ the unemployed.
　　A. for the benefit to　　　　　B. for the benefit of
　　C. for benefit of　　　　　　 D. for the benefit

(　　)10. The idea of _____ people comes naturally to most of us.
　　A. helping　　　B. help　　　C. to help　　　D. helps

(　　)11. —In English study, reading is more important than speaking, I think.
　　　—I don't agree with you. Speaking is _____ reading.
　　A. as important as　　　　　　B. so important as
　　C. the most important　　　　D. important than

(　　)12. They don't allow _____ in the building, but they allow me _____ out of it.
　　A. to smoke; smoking　　　　B. smoking; to smoke
　　C. to smoke; to smoke　　　　D. smoking; smoking

(　　)13. He's one of the best opponents I've _____ this season.

　　A. come over　　B. come after　　C. come along　　D. come across

(　　)14. A postcard, a present from my grandfather, would likely _____.

　　A. take one's eye　B. catch one's eye　C. get one's eyes　D. make one's eye

(　　)15. Life will become meaningful _____ we spend time helping others.

　　A. and　　B. though　　C. if　　D. unless

(　　)16. —Listen to my new CD I bought yesterday.

　　—Wow! That's totally _____!

　　A. lazy　　B. loud　　C. awesome　　D. handsome

(　　)17. Can the groups get people _____ trouble.

　　A. out of　　B. be out of　　C. out for　　D. be out from

(　　)18. Not only my two brothers but also my sister _____ watching TV.

　　A. like　　B. likes　　C. are like　　D. is like

(　　)19. Laying eggs _____ the ant queen's full-time job.

　　A. is　　B. are　　C. has　　D. have

(　　)20. If you think a letter is too slow, why not _____ a telegram?

　　A. try to have sent　　　　B. trying to send

　　C. to try to send　　　　　D. try sending

(　　)21. We should learn how _____ ourselves.

　　A. to protect　　B. protect　　C. protecting　　D. protected

(　　)22. The old woman has two daughters, one _____ is a teacher.

　　A. of them　　B. of which　　C. of whom　　D. of who

(　　)23. I've studied all the books _____ were borrowed from a library.

　　A. /　　B. that　　C. which　　D. what

(　　)24. We don't know the reason _____ he is always late.

　　A. for why　　B. why　　C. that　　D. which

(　　)25. Happiness often comes to those _____ work hard.

　　A. what　　B. which　　C. whom　　D. who

(　　)26. Have you found the woman _____ mobile phone was lost?

　　A. which　　B. of which　　C. whose　　D. that

(　　)27. He failed in the examination, _____ made his father very angry.

　　A. which　　B. it　　C. that　　D. what

(　　)28. A new shop _____ for a week nearby.

　　A. opened　　　　　　　　B. has been open

Unit 6 It's like a Home Away from Home

    C. has been opened   D. had been opened

(　　)29. I shall work _____ I can to help him.
  A. so hardly as B. as hardly as C. as hard as D. so hard as

(　　)30. His grade in the exam put him _____ the top students in his class.
  A. between B. over C. among D. above

第三节　完形填空:阅读下面的短文,从所给的A、B、C、D四个选项中选出正确的答案。(共10分,每小题1分)

  Mr. Turner's class planned to volunteer in the community service project. They had a discussion. The __31__ are some students' ideas. Mark, sitting in the front of the classroom __32__ that they could clean up the big park. Linda agreed with Mark. She suggested they __33__ some notices to tell people to keep the park tidy and __34__. Cara, as their monitor added that they had __35__ some money and they could buy notebooks and pencils for kids. __36__, some desks and chairs at our school were broken. They needed __37__ and they could help. Frank is __38__ clever than other students. He said that he had made a wonderful decision to go to the hospital to cheer up the sick children. In addition, some old people at the old people's home have much trouble __39__ the clothes. They could go there to help them. After the discussion stopped, Mr. Turner, their teacher said that he understood his students and all of their ideas were great. They would take a class vote(投票) to choose a community service project __40__ most students want to do.

(　　)31. A. following B. follow C. followed D. follows
(　　)32. A. talk B. thought C. speak D. went
(　　)33. A. put on B. put up C. put away D. put
(　　)34. A. clear B. dirty C. clean D. ugly
(　　)35. A. rose B. raising C. rising D raised
(　　)36. A. Except B. However C. Besides D. Except for
(　　)37. A. repair B. repaired C. repairing D. to repair
(　　)38. A. more B. much C. the most D. the better
(　　)39. A. washing B. wash C. to wash D. for washing
(　　)40. A. that B. it C. what D. when

第二部分　篇章与词汇理解(共分三节,满分50分)

第一节　阅读理解,阅读下列短文,从每题所给A、B、C、D四个选项中,选出最恰当的答案。(共30分,每小题2分)

A

  Community service means doing volunteer jobs for the public. It teaches valuable lessons

— 105 —

about the duties of a citizen(公民). Today, in the United States, important services are provided through thousands of organizations created to meet needs not provided by government at the local, state, and national levels. These activities help to create a sense of great care for the public.

There are close connections between community service programs and civic (公民的) education in schools. At every level of school, students can be involved in community service projects. In the primary grades, one of the purposes for students is to learn basic civic values that include fair play, respect for the opinions of others, and the duties of a citizen in our society.

By taking part in community service programs, every young child can learn how to solve problems, work in groups as leaders or group members, and accept the duties for their decisions and actions. Besides, children develop knowledge of their community—its leaders, organizations, social groups, and standards of civic behavior. Community service programs can provide the chances for students to learn social study skills. These include higher-level processes and skills of information collecting, critical thinking, and decision making. Community service programs also teach processes and skills for group discussions, leadership and teamwork.

Through community service programs, children can learn how people play roles in a discussion to work out the local problems. Students can volunteer to teach young children in child care centers or help in senior citizen centers.

(　　)41. From the passage, we know _____ play a main role in community service.

　　A. the adult citizens　　　　B. the volunteer organizations

　　C. the students at school　　D. the local and state governments

(　　)42. What is the meaning of the underlined sentence in Paragraph 2?

　　A. Children can learn about their community at school.

　　B. Civic education is about knowledge of community.

　　C. School students can offer community service programs.

　　D. Communities provide chances for school civic education.

(　　)43. Which of the following must be learnt in the primary grades?

　　A. Basic civic values.　　　　B. Social study processes.

　　C. Skills for information collecting.　　D. Processes of decision making.

(　　)44. What does the underlined word "These" in Paragraph 3 refer to?

　　A. The students.　　　　B. social study skills.

　　C. The chances.　　　　D. community service programs.

(　　)45. This passage is mainly about _____.

　　A. how the students set up community service organizations

　　B. how schools get involved in community service programs

C. what can be learnt by joining in community service projects

D. the volunteer jobs that the students can do in their community

B

Who do you admire? Different people may have different ideas.

If you're a sports fan, perhaps the person you admire most is a great basketball player, and Yao Ming is probably the one in your mind. If you study music or play an instrument, perhaps the person you admire most is gifted musician like Mozart, who began to write beautiful music at a very young age. Or maybe you admire great scientists, for example, Yuan Longping.

We have many reasons to admire famous people and we often give much of our respect to them. However, we shouldn't <u>neglect</u> those who are common, such as nurses, train drivers, firemen, cleaners and so on. They may be working in a corner of the world without being noticed, but all these people spend their working days serving the public. They show great dedication(奉献). However, what they do is often unnoticed by us. Have you ever thought our life will be like if they stop working?

So next time when you appreciate famous people, don't forget those who are common around you.

( ) 46. If you study music, perhaps the person you admire most is _____.

  A. Yao Ming   B. Mozart   C. Yuan Longping   D. Liu Xiang

( ) 47. The persons are common except _____.

  A. train drivers   B. cleaners   C. firemen   D. great scientists

( ) 48. The underlined word "neglect" in Paragraph 3 means _____.

  A. give comments on   B. make fun of

  C. Care about   D. pay no attention to

( ) 49. In Paragraph 3, the writer mainly points out _____.

  A. the reasons why we admire famous people

  B. the importance of common people's work

  C. the places where common people are working

  D. we often give much of our respect to famous people

( ) 50. What's the main idea of this passage?

  A. Famous people are admired by most of us in our life.

  B. Common people should also be given respect as the famous ones.

  C. Common people should be given the most respect in our society.

  D. Different people may have different ideas who we should admire.

C

A doctor was once teaching a class of medical students at a famous hospital in Edinburgh. An injured man was brought in, and the doctor turned to one of his students and asked him, "What's wrong with this man?"

"I don't know, Sir,"the student answered."Shall I examine him and find out?"

"There's no need to examine him," said the doctor. "You should know without asking questions. He has hurt his right knee. Didn't you notice the way he walked? He hurt it by burning it in the fire. You see his trousers leg is burnt away at the knee. This is Monday morning. Yesterday was fine, but on Saturday the roads were wet and muddy. The man's trousers are muddy all over. The man fell down on Saturday night."

The doctor then turned to the man and said, "You had your pay on Saturday and went to a public house and drank too much. You got muddy and wet on the way home. Because you had drunk too much, you fell on the fire and burnt your knee. Is that right?"

"Yes, sir."said the man.

( )51. The medical students were having a lesson _____.
  A. at the library   B. in a classroom
  C. at a well-known hospital   D. in a medical school

( )52. The man hurt his knee _____.
  A. on Monday   B. on Sunday night
  C. on Saturday night   D. yesterday

( )53. How did the doctor know that the man burnt his knee?
  A. From the way he walked.
  B. By seeing his trousers leg is burnt away at the knee.
  C. By seeing the man's trousers are muddy all over.
  D. Both A and B.

( )54. Which is the RIGHT order according to the passage?
  ① He burnt his knee. ② He got drunk. ③ He fell down and got muddy.
  ④ He had his pay.
  A. ①②③④   B. ④③②①   C. ③④①②   D. ④②③①

( )55. From the passage we know that _____ is very important for medical students.
  A. watching and thinking   B. taking good care of others
  C. learning from others   D. teaching

第二节　词义搭配:从(B)栏中选出(A)栏单词的正确解释。(共10分,每小题1分)

  (A)   (B)

( )56. benefit   A. to help a customer or sell them sth.

( )57. individual   B. events happen often

( )58. serve   C. things that are owned by sb.
( )59. committee   D. something that you are given for your hard work
( )60. property   E. a serious disease that often causes death
( )61. tailor   F. to be helpful or useful to
( )62. regularly   G. make sth. look more attractive
( )63. reward   H. a group of people who are chosen to deal with sth.
( )64. cancer   I. a person whose job is to make clothes
( )65. decorate   J. personal; one person

第三节 补全对话,根据对话内容,从对话后的选项中选出能填入空白处的最佳选项。(共 10 分,每小题 2 分)

A: Hi, Amy. __66__?

B: Hi, Tom. I am making some plans to volunteer in an old people's home.

A: Really? __67__?

B: A whole day. Would you like to come with me?

A: Yes. I'd like to. __68__?

B: There are many things we can do there, like reading the newspaper to the old, or just talking to them.

A: __69__. What else?

B: Well, a lot of old people are lonely. We should listen to them and care for them.

A: __70__. I believe we will have a meaningful day.

> A. I can't agree more.
> B. What are you doing?
> C. That sounds wonderful.
> D. What can we do to help them?
> E. How long do you plan to stay there?

第三部分 语言技能运用(共分四节,满分 30 分)

第一节 单词拼写:根据下列句子及所给汉语注释,在横线上写出单词的正确形式。(共 5 分,每小题 1 分)

71. It is an easy and _____(便利的) way to pass on love.

72. We always receive help from others, even from _____(陌生人).

73. After helping, we may _____(获得) more friends.

74. They join groups to share their _____(经验) with them.

75. The programme has built a strong _____（联系）among people.

第二节　词形变换：用括号内单词的适当形式填空，将正确答案写在横线上。（共 5 分，每小题 1 分）

76. If you want to _____（success）, always encourage yourself to do more.

77. She acted in the _____（believe）that she was doing good.

78. The competition is open to both teams and _____（individual）.

79. Nowadays, smartphones are _____（rely）on by lots of people.

80. Community _____（serve）makes it like a home away from home.

第三节　改错：从 A、B、C、D 四个画线处找出一处有错误的选项，并写出正确答案。（共 10 分，每小题 2 分）

81. I <u>don't know</u> <u>where</u> <u>have I seen</u> the man <u>before</u>.
　　　　A　　　　B　　　　C　　　　　　　D

82. It is <u>much</u> <u>easy</u> <u>to make</u> plans than to carry <u>them out</u>.
　　　　A　　B　　C　　　　　　　　　　D

83. <u>No one</u> <u>is allowed</u> <u>entering</u> the <u>big</u> hall.
　　　A　　　　B　　　　C　　　　D

84. We <u>saw</u> a lot <u>of boys</u> <u>on</u> the playground <u>played</u> football.
　　　A　　　　B　　　C　　　　　　　D

85. The book <u>which</u> I bought <u>it</u> last week was <u>written</u> <u>by</u> a famous writer.
　　　　　A　　　　　B　　　　　　C　　D

81.（　）应为_____　82.（　）应为_____　83.（　）应为_____

84.（　）应为_____　85.（　）应为_____

第四节　书面表达。（共 10 分）

作文题目：Learning from Lei Feng。

词数要求：80~100 词。

写作要点：(1)雷锋事迹和精神有很大影响；

(2)社区组织了学习雷锋的活动；

(3)你在生活中是如何帮助他人的？

Unit 7

High Technology Has Really Changed Our Life

Warming up

一、句型汇总

1. It's a good choice to ride a shared bicycle. 骑共享单车是一个好的选择。
2. The new energy vehicle is environmentally friendly. 新能源汽车是环保的。
3. The driverless car is a kind of intelligent vehicle. 无人驾驶汽车是一种智能汽车。
4. —What were you doing in this picture? 这张照片中你在做什么?
   —I was washing clothes by the river. 我在河边洗衣服。
5. You should take these tablets three times a day. 你需要吃这些药,一天三次。
6. High technology has really changed our life. 高科技确实改变了我们的生活。
7. Nowadays, lots of things can be done on the Internet. 如今,很多事情可以在互联网上完成。
8. Our life has changed so much because of high technology. 由于高科技,我们的生活发生了很大的变化。
9. The benefits of this decision are now obvious. 这个决定的好处现在是显而易见的。
10. This kind of life reminds me of the joy I felt when I was a kid. 这样的生活让我想起了我还是个孩子的时候所感受到的快乐。
11. Thus I've decided to make my short-term experiment longer. 因此,我决定延长我的短期实验。

12. The writer used to book movie tickets with a smartphone. 这位作家曾经用智能手机预订电影票。

13. It is convenient to settle a bill on a smartphone. 在智能手机上结账很方便。

14. I've never played tennis before, but I'll give it a shot. 我以前从未打过网球,但我会试一试。

15. Thanks to the power of artificial intelligence (AI), voice assistants will grow increasingly helpful. 英汉互译多亏了人工智能(AI)的影响力,语音助手将愈发有用。

二、英汉互译

1. high-speed train _____   2. 不再_____
3. shared bicycle _____   4. 电动牙刷_____
5. new energy vehicle _____ 6. 提醒某人做某事_____
7. driverless car _____   8. 对……着迷_____
9. cruise ship _____   10. 扫地机器人_____

Listening and Speaking

一、找出与所给单词画线部分读音相同的选项

( ) 1. appl<u>i</u>ance   A. <u>a</u>pply   B. <u>a</u>pplication   C. b<u>a</u>ttle   D. th<u>a</u>nks
( ) 2. trea<u>s</u>ure   A. great   B. plea<u>s</u>e   C. mea<u>s</u>ure   D. tea
( ) 3. <u>v</u>ehicle   A. negati<u>v</u>e   B. press   C. electric   D. e<u>v</u>erything
( ) 4. f<u>l</u>ow   A. power   B. fo<u>ll</u>ow   C. crowd   D. how
( ) 5. <u>ex</u>periment A. <u>ex</u>ample   B. <u>ex</u>hibit   C <u>ex</u>cerise   D. <u>ex</u>perience

二、从B栏中找出与A栏中相对应的答语

A

1. What are you doing on the Internet?
2. How did you keep in touch with your distant friends?
3. How long did it take you to return home?
4. Can you live without a smartphone for a week?
5. What can the robots do?

B

A. It can do almost all the housework.
B. Six hours.
C. By letter.
D. Sure.
E. I'm buying tickets to go home.

1. _____ 2. _____ 3. _____ 4. _____ 5. _____

Unit 7   High Technology Has Really Changed Our Life

三、补全对话

A: ___1___

B: Yes, there are a lot of technology productions which brought us so much convenience.

A: ___2___

B: Such as a car, it can save you much time by taking you to your destination, it's more convenient than it used to be.

A: Oh, yes, that's sure, especially the car could get up to 120 km/h on the expressway.

B: ___3___

A: Yes, you are right, so, ___4___

B: According to what I said above, car produced by technology could take your life away, and the traffic jams are also caused by so many cars.

A: ___5___

> A. But it could be very dangerous.
> B. Do you feel any convenience brought by high technology?
> C. Can you share your experience you had?
> D. Thank you very much!
> E. what's your opinion about the inconvenience brought by high technology?

四、场景模拟

编写一组英语对话,了解不同的火车票购买方式,和同学交流自己的购票经验。

提示词汇:online /Telephone Booking /Ticket Office /Primary Ticketing Company

_____
_____
_____
_____
_____
_____

Reading and Writing

一、用所给单词的适当形式填空

1. For me, friendship is one of the most precious _____ (珍宝) in the world.

2. Scientists have a fairly _____ (消极的) attitude to the theory.

3. _____ (因此), this problem should be solved by the following methods.

4. Her handshake was cool and _____ (结实的).

5. This question can be answered only by _____ (实验).

6. She _____ (unpack) all the clothes she needed and left the rest in the case.

7. Would you mind not _____ (interrupt) all the time?

8. People in this country _____ (joy) a high standard of living.

9. She _____ (press) her face against the window just now.

10. Your name has been _____ (delete) from the list.

二、完形填空

Technology has made life much easier for children today. It is __1__ for them to play, to listen to music, and to __2__ in touch with their friends. __3__ the help of technology, there seems to be nothing that children can't do now.

Technology also helps __4__ to know more about their children. For example, if a child is given a mobile phone with a tracking (追踪) device, his parents can find out __5__ he is going with the help of the mobile phone.

However, there are also some bad __6__ of technology. For example, it has become easier for bad people to get in touch with children with the help of technology. They can find personal information about children through special ways on the __7__. So it is very important for parents to __8__ their children to keep personal information safe while surfing the Internet.

Besides this, there is another bad thing about technology. Children now __9__ less time doing exercise than before. They are too __10__ playing online games. They can even play computer games all day long. If you don't push them out of the door, they won't volunteer to go out and play. This is not good for their health.

Therefore, teaching children the right way to make good use of technology is very important.

(   ) 1. A. easier　　　　B. more difficult　　C. more important　　D. harder
(   ) 2. A. lose　　　　　B. make　　　　　　C. keep　　　　　　　D. contact
(   ) 3. A. For　　　　　 B. Under　　　　　　C. With　　　　　　　D. Over
(   ) 4. A. teachers　　　B. friends　　　　　C. parents　　　　　　D. classmates
(   ) 5. A. when　　　　 B. whom　　　　　　C. why　　　　　　　D. where
(   ) 6. A. sides　　　　 B. places　　　　　　C. choices　　　　　　D. winds
(   ) 7. A. phone　　　　B. TV　　　　　　　C. radio　　　　　　　D. Internet
(   ) 8. A. teach　　　　 B. learn　　　　　　C. punish　　　　　　D. lend

Unit 7 High Technology Has Really Changed Our Life

(   )9. A. pay   B. take   C. cost   D. spend

(   )10. A. lazy   B. free   C. busy   D. hard-working

三、阅读理解

阅读下面短文,从每题所给的 A、B、C、D 四个选项中选出最佳答案

Perhaps you have heard a lot about the Internet, but what is it?

The Internet is many different networks around the world. A network is a group of computers that are put together. These networks joined together are called the Internet. Maybe that doesn't sound interesting. But when we've joined the Internet, there are lots of things we can do. We can have a lot of fun on the World Wide Web(www). We can use the Internet instead of a library to find all kinds of information for our homework. We can find information about our favorite sports or film stars and do shopping on the Internet. We can also send messages to other people by email. It is much cheaper and quicker than calling our friends or sending a letter.

With the help of the Internet, the world is becoming smaller and smaller. People can now work at home with a computer in front of them, getting and sending information. They can buy or sell the things that they want on the Internet. But do you know 98% of the information is in English? So what will English be like tomorrow?

(   )1. The passage is mainly about _____.

     A. the Internet   B. information   C. computers   D. email

(   )2. The quickest and cheapest way for people to send messages to their friends is _____.

     A. by post   B. by email   C. by telephone   D. by TV

(   )3. The Internet cannot be used to _____ according to the passage.

     A. find information for our homework

     B. get some information about our favorite sports stars

     C. do some shopping

     D. do our housework

(   )4. Which of the following is NOT true?

     A. The Internet is a big computer.

     B. The Internet is lots of computer networks.

     C. The Internet is very helpful.

     D. People can work at home with the help of the Internet.

(   )5. What does the writer try to tell us with the last two sentences?

     A. The Internet is more and more popular.

B. All the information is in English.

C. English is important in using the Internet.

D. Every computer must join the Internet.

四、书面表达

作文题目:Can Students Use Cell Phones?

词数要求:80~100 词。

写作要点:(1)手机的利弊;

(2)学生是否应该使用手机?

Grammar

一、从下面每小题四个选项中选出最佳选项

(　　)1. So far, many new gymnasiums _____ in the city.

  A. would be completed   B. was being completed

  C. have been completed   D. had been completed

(　　)2. I _____ TV at seven yesterday evening.

  A. am watching   B. watch   C. was watching   D. will watch

(　　)3. —Has he seen this film?

  —Yes. He _____ it five days ago.

  A. saw   B. has seen   C. had seen   D. was seeing

(　　)4. Great changes _____ in our country in the past ten years.

  A. have taken place   B. was taken place

  C. took place   D. have been taken place

(　　)5. It _____ heavily when I left my house.

Unit 7 High Technology Has Really Changed Our Life

    A. is raining   B. rains   C. was raining D. will rain

(　　)6. I shall tell you what he _____ at half past five yesterday afternoon.

    A. has done   B. has been done C. has been doing D. was doing

(　　)7. I _____ my work now.

    A. finished   B. finish   C. have finished D. had finished

(　　)8. _____ reading the book yet?

    A. Have you finished   B. Were you finishing

    C Had you finished   D. Are you finishing

(　　)9. The film _____ for five minutes.

    A. has begun   B. began   C. has on   D. has been on

(　　)10. —I'm sorry to keep you waiting.

    —Oh, not at all, I _____ here only a few minutes.

    A. have been   B. had been   C. had come   D. have come

(　　)11. —Did you go to England last month?

    —_____.

    A. No, I have never go there   B. No, I have never gone there

    C. No, I never was there   D. No, I have never been there

(　　)12. I _____ her since she was a little girl.

    A. knew   B. know   C. had known D. have known

(　　)13. Our teacher _____ to Beijing three times.

    A. went   B. had gone   C. has gone   D. has been

(　　)14. Last week, John _____ his leg.

    A. felt and broken   B. fell and broke

    C. feels and breaks   D. fallen and broken

(　　)15. —How long _____ to work there?

    —Since 2009.

    A. were you employed   B. have you been employed

    C. had you been employed   D. will you be employed

(　　)16. It _____ hard when we left.

    A. is raining   B. has rained   C. was raining D. rained

(　　)17. John said that he _____ his homework at seven yesterday.

    A. did   B. was doing   C. will do   D. has done

(　　)18. Would you please tell me where the nearest bank _____?

    A. was   B. is   C. will be   D. would be

— 117 —

( )19. He _____ quite a lot in his work.
   A. use to travel   B. is used to travel
   C. used to travel   D. was used to travel

( )20. It's eight years since I _____ my hometown.
   A. left   B. leave   C. have left   D. was leaving

( )21. His grandma has _____ for ten years.
   A. died   B. die   C. been dead   D. dead

( )22. It's the first time that she _____ Beijing.
   A. visits   B. visited   C. has visited   D. had visited

( )23. I _____ a college student for more than a year.
   A. became   B. have become   C. was   D. have been

( )24. I was very angry with John, he just _____ when I spoke to him.
   A. isn't listening   B. hasn't listened
   C. didn't listen   D. wasn't listening

( )25. When I came back yesterday evening, my brother _____ his homework.
   A. is doing B. has done   C. was doing   D. had done

( )26. Our teacher told us the sun _____ in the east.
   A. rose   B. rises   C. is rising   D. was rising

( )27. The telephone _____, but by the time I got indoors, it stopped.
   A. had rung B. was ringing   C. rings   D. has rung

( )28. I called John many times yesterday evening, but I couldn't get through. His brother _____ on the phone all the time!
   A. was talking   B. has been talking
   C. has talked   D. talked

( )29. I don't believe you've already finished reading the book. I _____ it to you this morning!
   A. would lend   B. was lending   C. had lent   D. lent

( )30. —Have you read a book called *Waiting for Anya*?
       —Who _____ it?
   A. writes   B. has written   C. wrote   D. had written

二、找出下列句子中错误的选项,并改正过来

1. When I came in, he is sleeping inside.
      A   B   C   D

Unit 7　High Technology Has Really Changed Our Life

2. Great changes have been taken place in my hometown since 2008.
　　　　A　　　B　　　　C　　　　　　　　　　　　D

3. It's said that Jim's grandpa has died for ten years.
　　A　　B　　C　　　　　　　　D

4. What were they do to my computer just now?
　　A　　B　　C　　　　　　　　D

5. As a lot of trees have cut, birds have no place to build their homes.
　A　　　　　　　B　　　　　　　　　　　　C　　D

6. She said he has a beautiful doll.
　A　　B　　C　　　　　D

7. Could you tell me where the hospital was?
　　　　　　A　　B　　C　　　　　D

8. I didn't hear the phone. I must be asleep.
　　　A　　B　　　　　　　　　　C　　D

9. We often played together when we are children.
　　　　A　　　B　　　　C　　D

10. Robert has arrived in England a few weeks ago.
　　　　　　A　　　B　　　　　C　　　　D

More Activities

一、找出与所给单词画线部分读音相同的选项

(　　) 1. thus　　A. rubber　　B. flu　　C. suppose　　D. communication

(　　) 2. digital　　A. fibre　　B. library　　C. distant　　D. remind

(　　) 3. high-tech　　A. Christmas　　B. children　　C. catch　　D. check

(　　) 4. focus　　A. uniform　　B. university　　C. unhappy　　D. upon

(　　) 5. therefore　　A. breathe　　B. throughout　　C. thought　　D. thirsty

二、英汉互译

1. 远离_____　　　　2. communicate with _____

3. 使(某人)想起_____　　4. do harm to _____

5. 集中(注意力)于_____　　6. spend...on _____

7. 接力赛_____　　　　8. digital books _____

9. 支持_____　　　　10. thanks to _____

三、用所给单词的适当形式填空

1. For the past decade or so, high _____ (technical) has been changing the way we live.

— 119 —

2. Can you come at 10.30? I know it's _____ (convenient) for you, but I must see you.

3. With high technology, people tend to spend less time _____ (communicate) with each other face to face.

4. It will be _____ (harm) to our eyes to spend too much time on digital books.

5. Add more arguments to support your _____ (favour) side.

6. It has proved _____ (effect) as a training tool to educate drivers about the dangers of bad driving.

7. Voice assistants can do a _____ (vary) of things after hearing a wake-up word or command.

8. Young men can easily get _____ (hook) on this kind of music.

9. Her younger brother was the _____ (favour) child, encouraged and admired by both parents.

10. Will new technology change the shape of _____ (broadcast)?

四、找出下列句子中错误的选项,并改正过来

1. People tend to rely too much in high technology.
   　　　　　A　 B　　　C　　　D

2. Some people think it makes our life more convenient, when others hold the opposite view.
   　　　　　　　　A　B　　　　　　C　　　　　　D

3. It's convenience to make video calls.
   　A　　B　　　C　　　D

4. Britain is not longer in the front rank of world powers.
   　　　A B　　　　C　　　　　　　　D

5. I was used to smoke but I gave up two years ago.
   　A　　B　　C　　　　　　　　　　D

单元检测

第一部分　英语知识运用(共分三节,满分40分)

第一节　语音知识:从 A、B、C、D 四个选项中找出画线部分与所给单词画线部分读音相同的选项。(共5分,每小题1分)

(　　)1. interrupted　　A. favoured　　B. finished　　C. visited　　D. prepared

(　　)2. vehicle　　A. diligence　　B. company　　C. center　　D. cinema

(　　)3. obvious　　A. focus　　B. opportunity　　C. hole　　D welcome

Unit 7 High Technology Has Really Changed Our Life

( )4. granny   A. widely   B. recycle   C. yellow   D. style

( )5. accident   A. account   B. accomplish   C. success   D. according

第二节 词汇与语法知识:从 A、B、C、D 四个选项中选出可以填入空白处的最佳选项。(共 25 分,每小题 1 分)

( )6. Don't forget to keep _____ touch with your teachers and classmates after you graduate.

　　A. on   B. in   C. by   D. through

( )7. Mr White used to _____ in China, so he gets used to _____ Chinese dishes.

　　A. live; eating   B. live; eat   C. living; eating   D. living; eat

( )8. Our life has changed so much _____ high technology.

　　A. so that   B. such that   C. because   D. because of

( )9. The old photo _____ me _____ my childhood.

　　A. reminds...of   B. regards...of   C. reminds...to   D. regards...to

( )10. Sorry to _____, but there's someone to see you.

　　A. stop   B. prevent   C. interrupt   D. keep

( )11. The talks will _____ economic development of the region.

　　A. insist on   B. focus on   C. rely on   D. show on

( )12. He could _____ hold back his tears.

　　A. not longer   B. no longer   C. not more   D. no more

( )13. I _____ help you as possible as l can.

　　A. am willing to   B. be willing to   C. willing to   D. willing

( )14. —_____ you _____ your homework yet?

　　— Yes. I _____ it a moment ago.

　　A. Did; do; finished   B. Have; done; finished

　　C. Have; done; have finished   D. Did; do; have finished

( )15. My father _____ to Beijing last year. He _____ there several times before.

　　A. has gone; had been   B. went; had gone

　　C. went; had been   D. went; went

( )16. _____ the Internet, mail is now instantly available.

　　A. Thanks   B. Thanks to   C. Thanks for   D. because

( )17. After so many years, she was still _____ recognizable.

　　A. instantly   B. straight   C. quick   D. slowly

( )18. With high technology, people _____ spend less time communicating with each

— 121 —

other face to face.

　　　　A. tend to　　　B. add to　　　C. lead to　　　D. fail to

(　　)19. Young men can easily _____ this kind of music.

　　　　A. get attracted on　　　　　　B. get addicted on
　　　　C. get hooked on　　　　　　　D. get used to

(　　)20. Eating _____ sugar can lead to health problems.

　　　　A. many too　　B. too many　　C. much too　　D. too much

(　　)21. Engineers spend much time and energy _____ brilliant solutions.

　　　　A. develop　　B. developing　　C. developed　　D. on developing

(　　)22. Reading in a dim light can be _____ the eyes.

　　　　A. harm to　　B. harmful to　　C. harm for　　D. harmful for

(　　)23. The system has the ability _____ more than one programme at the same time.

　　　　A. to running　　B. running　　C. to run　　D. run

(　　)24. He thought he would benefit _____ going to school.

　　　　A. from　　　　B. in　　　　C. on　　　　D. with

(　　)25. It is rude to _____ other people.

　　　　A. watch　　　B. look　　　C. look at　　　D. stare at

(　　)26. _____ the Air Purifier off at any time, press the power button and all indicator lights will go off.

　　　　A. Turning　　B. Turned　　C. To turn　　D. Turn

(　　)27. Younger generations may forget how _____ words and write correctly.

　　　　A. to spell　　B. spelling　　C. spell　　D. to spelling

(　　)28. —Do you know him well?

　　　　—Sure. We _____ friends since ten years ago.

　　　　A. were　　B. have been　　C. have become　　D. became

(　　)29. _____ your father _____ at this time yesterday?

　　　　A. Was; working　B. Is; working　C. Did; work　D. Has; worked

(　　)30. Many people do not like the idea of _____ on animals.

　　　　A. exam　　B. experiment　　C. experience　　D. exercises

第三节　完形填空：阅读下面的短文，从所给的 A、B、C、D 四个选项中选出最佳的答案。(共 10 分，每小题 1 分)

James Dyson is a famous British inventor. One of his well-known inventions is the bagless vacuum cleaner (真空吸尘器). He __31__ it in 1978. Today Dyson still __32__ that day. "I was the only man in the world with a bagless vacuum cleaner!" he said.

Unit 7　High Technology Has Really Changed Our Life

Dyson, 65, wasn't a(n) __33__ at first. When he studied art at the Royal College of Art in London, he began to show an interest in design. There he invented his first product, the Sea Truck. It was a boat for __34__ anything between islands.

Then he started his first company to make and sell __35__ invention. The Ballbarrow is a kind of vehicle (交通工具). But later Dyson left his __36__. He didn't agree with his partners.

After that Dyson began to improve on the vacuum cleaner. In 1985, Dyson took his product to Japan and __37__ the Japanese to sell it. However, he didn't make much money. Several years later Dyson decided to __38__ and sell the machine himself. By 2005, Dyson controlled both the European and American __39__.

Along the way, Dyson discovered the secret of __40__. "People will buy products if they're better".

(　　)31. A. discovered　　B. invented　　C. produced　　D. found
(　　)32. A. remembers　　B. forgets　　C. notices　　D. tastes
(　　)33. A. engineer　　B. teacher　　C. listener　　D. soldier
(　　)34. A. taking　　B. fetching　　C. carrying　　D. bringing
(　　)35. A. other　　B. the other　　C. another　　D. others
(　　)36. A. company　　B. circle　　C. country　　D. research
(　　)37. A. hoped　　B. made　　C. allowed　　D. supported
(　　)38. A. produce　　B. divide　　C. create　　D. throw
(　　)39. A. baskets　　B. markets　　C. websites　　D. organizations
(　　)40. A. happiness　　B. success　　C. failure　　D. sadness

第二部分　篇章与词汇理解(共分三节,满分50分)

第一节　阅读理解,阅读下列短文,从每题所给的 A、B、C、D 四个选项中,选出最恰当的答案。(共30分,每小题2分)

A

Having a smart phone may not be as smart as you think. They may let you surf the Internet, listen to music and take photos wherever you are…but they also turn you into a workaholic(工作狂),it seems.

A study suggests that, by giving you access to emails at all times, the smart phone adds as much as two hours to your working day. Experts found that British people work an additional 460 hours a year on average as they are able to respond to emails on their mobiles. The study shows the average UK working day is between 9 and 10 hours, but 2 more hours is spent responding to or sending work emails, or making work calls.

Almost one in ten admits spending up to three hours outside their normal working day checking work emails. Some workers say they are on call almost 24 hours a day. Nearly two-thirds say they often check work emails just before they go to bed and as soon as they wake up, while over a third have replied to one in the middle of the night. The average time for first checking emails is between 6 a.m and 7 a.m, with more than a third checking their first email in the period, and a quarter checking them between 11 p.m. and midnight.

Ghadi Hobeika, marketing director of Pixmania, said: "The ability to access millions of Apps has made smart phone <u>invaluable</u> for many people. However, there are disadvantages. Many companies expect their employees to be on call 24 hours a day, seven days a week, and smart phones mean that people cannot get away from work. The more frequently in contact we become, the more is expected of us in a work capacity."

( )41. With a smart phone, the average UK working day is _____.
    A. 11 to 12 hours   B. 9 to 10 hours
    C. 8 hours   D. 2 hours

( )42. We can learn from the text that the British people _____.
    A. prefer to check emails in the morning
    B. are crazy about different smart phone
    C. work more hours with smart phones
    D. shorten their normal working hours

( )43. What does the underlined word "invaluable" mean?
    A. useless   B. necessary   C. expensive   D. cheap

( )44. Where can we most probably read this text?
    A. In a science fiction.   B. In a newspaper.
    C. In a travel magazine.   D. In a storybook.

( )45. What does Ghadi Hobeika feel about smart phones?
    A. They are unimportant for most of people.
    B. They have disadvantages for some companies.
    C. They are useful to improve a work ability.
    D. They make it impossible for people to rest.

B

Technology can help keep animals out of Japan's farms. Scientists have made the "Super Monster Wolf" to scare away wild animals. The solar-powered robot looks real. It has wolf-like hair, scary teeth and red eyes. It also has 48 different wolf howls(嗥叫) so animals can't get used to it. Farms have lost millions of dollars every year because of hungry animals before. The

Unit 7　High Technology Has Really Changed Our Life

robot will keep wild pigs and deer out of rice fields, farms and fruit gardens.

　　Some Japan's experts tested the robot in nine places. It is said that the robot really reduced crop losses(损失) and was better than electric fences at keeping animals out. The robot senses movement up to one kilometer away. The 65 cm-long robot will be sold from next month. The price is ＄4,800 but farmers can rent it by the month. Japan's farmers hope this new electronic wolf will stop wild animals eating their crops.

(　　)46. What's the meaning of the underlined phases "scare away" in Chinese?
　　　　A. 吓跑　　　　B. 保护　　　　C. 搜索　　　　D. 追逐

(　　)47. What does the first paragraph mainly tell us?
　　　　A. How to make a solar-powered robot.
　　　　B. The solar-powered robot looks real.
　　　　C. There are lots of hungry animals in the fields.
　　　　D. The "Super Monster Wolf" can scare away animals.

(　　)48. Farms have lost lots of money every year because of _____.
　　　　A. the bad weather　　　　　　B. the "Super Monster Wolf"
　　　　C. hungry animals　　　　　　D. all kinds of robots

(　　)49. How long is "Super Monster Wolf"?
　　　　A. 62cm　　　　B. 63cm　　　　C. 64cm　　　　D. 65cm

(　　)50. What's the Japan's farmers wish?
　　　　A. Wild animals will never eat their crops.
　　　　B. The robot senses movement up to one kilometer away.
　　　　C. Farmers can rent the robot.
　　　　D. Technology can help keep animals out of Japan's farms.

C

　　The computer is a useful machine. It is the most important invention in many years. The oldest kind of computer is the abacus(算盘), used in China centuries ago, but the first large, modern computer was built in 1946. A computer then could do maths problems quite fast.

　　Today computers are used in many ways and can do many kinds of work. In a few years, the computer may touch the life of everyone, even people in faraway villages.

　　In the last few years, there have been great changes in computers. They are getting smaller and smaller, and computing faster and faster, Many scientists agree that computers can now do many things, but they cannot do everything. Who knows what the computers of tomorrow will be like? Will computers bring good things or bad things to people? The scientists of today will have to decide how to use the computers of tomorrow.

(   )51. The computer is a _____ machine.
        A. helpful   B. strange   C. large   D. dangerous

(   )52. The first large, modern computer was built about _____ years ago.
        A. a few   B. forty   C. sixty   D. seventy

(   )53. The computers of today are _____ than before.
        A. bigger   B. fewer   C. smaller   D. taller

(   )54. Computers can do _____.
        A. everything   B. anything   C. nothing   D. lots of things

(   )55. The scientists of today _____ how to use the computers of tomorrow.
        A. may decide   B. must decide
        C. can make   D. needn't make

第二节 词义搭配:从(B)栏中选出(A)栏单词的正确解释。(共10分,每小题1分)

                (A)   (B)

(   )56. interrupt   A. to help sb. remember sth.
(   )57. experiment   B. far away
(   )58. benefit   C. the mother of your father or mother
(   )59. immediate   D. a scientific test
(   )60. remind   E. to say or do sth that makes sb stop what they are saying or doing
(   )61. unpack   F. cars, buses, trucks, etc.
(   )62. delete   G. an advantage that sth. gives you
(   )63. granny   H. to remove sth. that has been written or printed
(   )64. vehicle   I. to take things out of a suitcase, bag, etc.
(   )65. distant   J. instant; at once

第三节 补全对话,根据对话内容,从对话后的选项中选出能填入空白处的最佳选项。(共10分,每小题2分)

Clerk: Onxiu Travel Agency. May I help you?

Jia Xiang: Yes, __66__

Clerk: Your name, please.

Jia Xiang: Jia Xiang. __67__

Clerk: Let me see what's available…Yes, Air China has a flight on May 5th at 9:15 in the morning.

Jia Xiang: Well, __68__

Clerk: Single ticket or return ticket?

Jia Xiang: Single. __69__

Unit 7　High Technology Has Really Changed Our Life

Clerk：Economy fare for single ticket from Beijing to Shanghai is 500 *yuan*.

Jia Xiang：I see. Is my ticket confirmed then?

Clerk：__70__. Please arrive at the airport one hour before departure.

Jia Xiang：Thank you.

> A. What's the fare, please?
> B. I'd like to make a plane reservation to Shanghai China.
> C. I need an economy ticket.
> D. Yes, your seat is confirmed on that flight.
> E. I'd like to leave on May 5th.

第三部分　语言技能运用(共分四节,满分30分)

第一节　单词拼写：根据下列句子及所给汉语注释,在横线上写出单词的正确形式。(共5分,每小题1分)

71. You would be in _____ (支持、赞成) of his coming, wouldn't you?

72. I've never cooked this before, so it's an _____ (实验).

73. China sent a man into space in this _____ (宇宙飞船).

74. Positive and _____ (消极的) experiences form a child's character.

75. _____ (如今), most kids prefer watching TV to reading.

第二节　词形变换：用括号内单词的适当形式填空,将正确答案写在横线上。(共5分,每小题1分)

76. I thought he was very attractive and _____ (obvious) very clever.

77. They were _____ (interrupt) by a knock at the door.

78. _____ (distant) is no problem on the Internet.

79. Our life has changed so much because of high _____ (technical).

80. The girl's question _____ (remind) Mr Wu of something he had read somewhere before.

第三节　改错：从A、B、C、D四个画线处找出一处有错误的选项,并写出正确答案。(共10分,每小题2分)

81. Her parents <u>not</u> <u>longer</u> have any real <u>influence</u> <u>over</u> her.
　　　　　　　　A　　　B　　　　　　　　C　　　　D

82. Our teachers often tell us <u>don't</u> to get <u>hooked</u> <u>on</u> <u>the</u> online gaming.
　　　　　　　　　　　　　　A　　　　　B　　C　D

83. <u>Own</u> a car <u>like</u> this <u>is</u> <u>many</u> men's dream.
　　A　　　　　B　　　C　　D

84. His father has joined the Party since 1978.
          A   B   C   D
85. Too much wine can do harmful to one's health.
         A   B   C   D

81.( )应为_____ 82.( )应为_____ 83.( )应为_____
84.( )应为_____ 85.( )应为_____

第四节　书面表达。(共 10 分)

作文题目:Technology and Life。

词数要求:80~100 词。

Unit 8

I Have a Dream

Warming up

一、句型汇总

1. —What do you want to do after graduation? 你毕业之后想要做什么?

—I want to work as an auto salesman for a big company. 我想在一家大公司做汽车销售。

2. —Have you prepared for your dream? 你为你的梦想做好准备了吗?

—I think I have. 我想我准备好了。

3. —Do you have a dream? 你有梦想吗?

—Of course, I'd like to find a job which involves food. 当然有了,我想要找一份和食物有关的工作。

4. Hopefully your dream will come true one day. 希望有一天你能梦想成真。

5. It was a lucky day for me because I learnt a lesson I will never forget. 对我来说,这是幸运的一天,因为我学到了终生难忘的一课。

6. He was keen on repairing cars and good at it. 他喜爱修车并擅长于此。

7. Wu Wei was a careful and responsible person. 吴伟是一个细心、负责的人。

8. From the story I learnt that one can become outstanding in his field as long as he has a dream and works hard at it. 从这个故事中我学到,一个人只要有梦想并为之努力奋斗,就可以

在自己的工作领域中做得很出色。

9. The important thing is to know what you want, and then do everything you can to realise your dream. 重要的是知道你想要什么,然后尽你所能去实现你的梦想。

10. His performance at the forum was outstanding. 他在论坛的表现非常出色。

11. Whatever we do, we should make an effort. 无论我们做什么,我们都应该努力。

12. We all have dreams, big or small. 我们都有或大或小的梦想。

13. You should be more confident to realise your dream. 你应该更有信心实现你的梦想。

14. The most important thing is to believe in yourself. 最重要的是相信自己。

15. Clear your mind of all negative thoughts and think positively. 清除你所有消极的想法,积极思考。

16. The power of positive thinking can improve your life and help you realise your dream. 积极思考的力量可以改善你的生活,帮助你实现你的梦想。

17. My dream is to work as a tour guide at a travel agency. 我的梦想是在旅行社担任导游。

二、英汉互译

1. lose some weight _____   2. 练习做…… _____
3. fly in a hot-air balloon _____   4. 克服我的恐惧 _____
5. have an opportunity _____   6. 采取行动 _____
7. doing more exercise _____   8. 抓住机遇 _____
9. gain related knowledge _____   10. 努力学习 _____

Listening and Speaking

一、找出与所给单词画线部分读音相同的选项

(   )1. photogr<u>a</u>phy   A. <u>a</u>pply   B. <u>a</u>pplication   C. <u>a</u>vailable   D. <u>a</u>ccept

(   )2. rec<u>o</u>mmend   A. c<u>o</u>mmunication B. c<u>o</u>mmon   C. <u>o</u>pportunity   D. <u>o</u>pen

(   )3. hopef<u>u</u>lly   A. <u>u</u>niversity   B. l<u>u</u>ck   C. l<u>u</u>cky   D. poll<u>u</u>tion

(   )4. <u>e</u>nvy   A. Chin<u>e</u>se   B. sp<u>e</u>ll   C. dr<u>e</u>am   D. th<u>e</u>se

(   )5. sugges<u>tion</u>   A. gradua<u>tion</u>   B. ques<u>tion</u>   C. collec<u>tion</u>   D. situa<u>tion</u>

二、从 B 栏中找出与 A 栏中相对应的答语

A

1. Did you have a beautiful dream when you was a little girl?
2. Where are you going to work?
3. I hope your dream will come true.
4. How are you going to become a teacher?
5. Have you prepared for your dream?

B

A. I'm going to work in a school in the poor village.
B. I think I have.
C. I'm going to study hard and do well in all the subjects.
D. Thanks.
E. Sure, I definitely had a lot of beautiful dreams when I was a young girl.

1. _____ 2. _____ 3. _____ 4. _____ 5. _____

三、补全对话

A：I believe that everyone in the world has his own dream, so do I.

B： 1

A：In my childhood, my dream was to be a policeman.

B：Why?

A：Because I have watched police on the TV. So cool.

B： 2

A：No. But when I grow up, I have another dream.

B： 3

A：I want to be a writer.

B：Why do you change your dream when you grow up?

A：Because writing can help me describe many kinds of lives and also can help me remember some important memories in my life.

B：Ok. 4

A：I guess I like it. Because I want to read books. 5 Sometimes, I like writing some articles.

B：What are you going to do now?

A：I am thinking about to be a writer in the future. That's all my dream and plan. Thank you!

A. What is your another dream?
B. Are you a policeman now?
C. I think reading books is an interesting thing.
D. What is your dream?
E. Do you like to write stuff?

四、场景模拟

编写一组英语对话,和同学谈论自己的梦想。

提示词汇:dream of doing / want to be / it sounds cool / opportunities favor prepared mind/ come true

_____

_____

_____

_____

_____

_____

Reading and Writing

一、用所给单词的适当形式填空

1. He is a _____(技工)who buys and sells cars on the side.

2. She gained only minimal _____(赞誉)for her work.

3. He volunteered to serve as the manager of our _____(部、系)store.

4. Derartu is an _____(杰出的)athlete and deserved to win.

5. Helen is a very well-known _____(小说家)in Australia.

6. She made a good _____(impress)on the interviewer.

7. _____(employ)usually decide within five minutes whether someone is suitable for the job.

8. I was pleased to hear you've been _____(promote).

9. As parents, you should shoulder your _____(response).

10. He is used to being _____(recognition)in the street.

二、完形填空

Everybody dreams. Some people think dreams can tell us about the future. Other people think dreams tell us about ourselves. It's like our __1__ is talking to us. Why are dreams __2__ strange and hard to understand? Some people think our brain uses __3__ to talk to us. When we fly, swim, or fall down in our dreams, it has a __4__ meaning. Lots of doctors help people __5__ their dreams. They find that dreams tell us about our __6__ and fears.

These days, many scientists __7__ that dreams are very important. During the day, we have many __8__, and our brain receives a lot of information. When we dream, our brain __9__ information that is not important, and puts the most important information into our __10__. As we learn more about the brain, we may find answers to our questions about dreams.

( ) 1. A. body   B. spirit   C. brain   D. heart
( ) 2. A. never   B. seldom   C. ever   D. often
( ) 3. A. symbols   B. examples   C. numbers   D. pictures
( ) 4. A. special   B. serious   C. similar   D. great
( ) 5. A. finish   B. forget   C. understand   D. continue
( ) 6. A. hopes   B. rights   C. positions   D. abilities
( ) 7. A. reply   B. believe   C. doubt   D. worry
( ) 8. A. experiences   B. dreams   C. mistakes   D. inventions
( ) 9. A. passes on   B. looks into   C. throws away   D. asks for
( ) 10. A. feelings   B. stories   C. lives   D. memories

三、阅读理解

阅读下面短文，从每题所给的 A、B、C、D 四个选项中选出最佳答案

Once upon a time, there was a tree which wanted to become a treasure box. One day, a farmer cut it down and sold it to a <u>carpenter</u>. The tree was happy because he thought the carpenter would make it into a treasure box.

To its surprise, the carpenter made it into a feed box for animals. The tree felt very disappointed because that was not its dream. Several years later, the feed box was thrown away. Someone picked it up and placed it into an old temple. The tree forgot its dream little by little.

One day, a couple came to the temple. The woman gave birth to a baby boy. There wasn't a bed in the temple. So they placed the baby in the feed box. They loved him and regarded him as their treasure. The tree suddenly realized that it became a real "treasure box" at that time.

Sometimes you may think your dream will not come true. Don't forget your dream. It may be realized in another new way.

(　　)1. Why the tree was happy when the farmer sold it to a carpenter?

　　A. Because the tree thought the carpenter would make it into a treasure box.

　　B. Because his owner would be richer.

　　C. Because he thought he was valuable.

　　D. Because he wanted to be a feed box.

(　　)2. What's the tree's dream?

　　A. To be a feed box.　　　　　　B. To be a treasure box.

　　C. To be thrown away.　　　　　D. To be sold.

(　　)3. Why the couple used the feed box as their baby's bed?

　　A. They thought the feed box is comfortable.

　　B. There wasn't a bed in the temple.

　　C. Their baby asked them to do so.

　　D. The feed box is clean.

(　　)4. What's the meaning of the underlined word in the first paragraph.

　　A. 商人　　　B. 律师　　　C. 木匠　　　D. 教授

(　　)5. What does the author want to tell us?

　　A. Don't forget your dream. It may be realized in another new way.

　　B. Failure is the mother of success.

　　C. Where there is a will, there is a way.

　　D. Practice makes perfect.

四、书面表达

作文题目：My Dream。

词数要求：80~100 词。

写作要点：(1)你的梦想是什么？

(2)把此作为梦想的原因是什么？

Unit 8 I Have a Dream

Grammar

一、从下面每小题四个选项中选出最佳选项

(   ) 1. We did not expect our offer _____ so quickly.
      A. rejected   B. to rejected   C. to be rejected   D. rejecting

(   ) 2. He told her _____ there at once.
      A. get   B. gets   C. should get   D. to get

(   ) 3. Paul does nothing but _____ all day long.
      A. play   B. to play   C. playing   D. played

(   ) 4. I don't know her and I don't _____.
      A. want   B. want to   C. want it   D. to want

(   ) 5. To play fair is as important as _____.
      A. to play well   B. play well   C. we play well   D. playing well

(   ) 6. It's very foolish _____ it.
      A. for you to say   B. of you to say   C. with you saying   D. in your saying

(   ) 7. It _____ me two hours to find your new house.
      A. cost   B. took   C. spent   D. used

(   ) 8. I really don't know _____.
      A. to swim   B. how to swim   C. to swim how   D. how swim

(   ) 9. Her parents won't let her _____ out with her boyfriend.
      A. goes   B. to go   C. going   D. go

(   ) 10. —Go to the theatre with me, will you?
      —I would like _____, but I don't have time.
      A. to   B. too   C. to do   D. to go to

(   ) 11. I asked him _____ with us.
      A. when to go   B. when he will go
      C. if he will go   D. that he would go

(   ) 12. Don't forget _____ the newspaper when you have finished it.
      A. putting back   B. pat back   C. to put back   D. be put back

(   ) 13. He asked me _____ a noise in the office.
      A. not to make   B. to not make   C. don't make   D. not making

(   ) 14. She prefers _____ rather than _____.
      A. die; give in   B. die; to give in

C. to die; give in   D. to die; to give in

( ) 15. We should learn how _____ ourselves.
A. to protect   B. protect   C. protecting   D. protected

( ) 16. Are you going to attend the meeting _____ next Saturday?
A. holding   B. hold   C. to hold   D. to be held

( ) 17. _____ the project on time, the staff were working at weekends.
A. Completing   B. Having completed
C. To have completed   D. To complete

( ) 18. The play _____ next month aims mainly to reflect the local culture.
A. produced   B. being produced
C. to be produced   D. having been produced

( ) 19. He told us whether _____ a picnic was still under discussion.
A. to have   B. having   C. have   D. had

( ) 20. We are invited to a party _____ in our club next Friday.
A. to be held   B. held   C. being held   D. holding

( ) 21. Tom could do nothing but _____ to his teacher that he was wrong.
A. admit   B. admitted   C. admitting   D. to admit

( ) 22. He arrived at the station, only _____ the train had left.
A. finding   B. find   C. to find   D. found

( ) 23. It takes me half an hour _____ the piano every day.
A. play   B. playing   C. to play   D. played

( ) 24. The teacher asked those boys _____ too much noise in class.
A. do not make   B. not make   C. not making   D. not to make

( ) 25. We have worked for three hours. Now let's stop _____ a rest.
A. had   B. have   C. to have   D. having

( ) 26. The boy is often heard _____ in the music room. He sings very well.
A. practice singing   B. to practice singing
C. practiced singing   D. to practice to sing

( ) 27. Let him _____ a rest. I think he must be tired after the long walk.
A. has   B. have   C. to have   D. having

( ) 28. The old man was _____ angry _____ say a word.
A. so; that   B. as; as   C. too; to   D. very; to

( ) 29. Why _____ home tomorrow?
A. not go   B. not going   C. not to go   D. didn't go

( ) 30. It's cold outside. You had better _____ your coat.
A. to put on   B. putting on   C. puts on   D. put on

Unit 8　I Have a Dream

二、找出下列句子中错误的选项，并改正过来

1. I have no choice but wait for him.
   　　A　　　　B　　C　D

2. His parents encourage him speaking loudly.
   　　A　　　B　　　　C　　D

3. In order to not lose her job, she asked the manager to reduce her salary for the accident.
   　　A　　　　　　　　B　　　　　　C　　　　　　D

4. Remember calling me as soon as you get home.
   　A　　　B　　　C　　　D

5. He was too tired not to walk any further.
   　　　A　　B　　　C　　D

6. To answer correctly is more important than finishing quickly.
   　　　　　A　B　　　　　　C　　D

7. Try to not depend on others.
   A　B　　C　　D

8. You'd better not to be late for class again.
   　　A　　B C　D

9. No one is allowed entering the big hall.
   　A　　B　　　C　　　D

10. I would like know the reason why you're so late.
    　A　　　B　　　　C　　　D

More Activities

一、找出与所给单词画线部分读音相同的选项

(　) 1. unk<u>n</u>own　　A. <u>p</u>ower　　B. flo<u>w</u>er　　C. all<u>ow</u>　　D. narr<u>ow</u>

(　) 2. m<u>u</u>sician　　A. <u>u</u>niversity　　B. bl<u>u</u>e　　C. <u>u</u>nnecessary　　D. <u>u</u>pon

(　) 3. h<u>o</u>ckey　　A. m<u>o</u>ney　　B. pil<u>o</u>t　　C. h<u>o</u>me　　D. <u>o</u>pportunity

(　) 4. si<u>n</u>ger　　A. lo<u>n</u>g　　B. ora<u>n</u>ge　　C. autum<u>n</u>　　D. u<u>n</u>kind

(　) 5. <u>c</u>linic　　A. pi<u>c</u>nic　　B. <u>c</u>inema　　C. <u>c</u>entury　　D. audien<u>c</u>e

二、英汉互译

1. 遨游太空 _____

2. take good care of _____

3. 开诊所 _____

4. come true _____

5. 学会一种乐器 _____

6. discuss…with _____

7. 对……感兴趣 _____

8. dream of doing _____

9. 导游 _____

10. land on _____

— 137 —

三、用所给单词的适当形式填空

1. The Dream Factory is the largest all-volunteer driven children's wish-granting _____ (organise).

2. As a common member of these _____ (audience), it is so lucky for me that I can go on television.

3. I'm _____ (interest) in animation.

4. My major is travel and _____ (tour).

5. We _____ (grateful) accepted his promise to help us.

6. I told myself I would be _____ (satisfy) with whatever I could get.

7. I didn't want to go but he _____ (insist).

8. She has always _____ (envy) my success.

9. _____ (hopeful) I can open a company like you one day.

10. He lay in the darkness, _____ (pretend) to sleep.

四、找出下列句子中错误的选项,并改正过来

1. She pretended not seeing me when I passed by.
        A   B   C   D

2. I will go to school as long as it won't rain tomorrow.
     A   B   C   D

3. I prefer do some sports rather than stay at home.
     A B   C   D

4. Believe it or no, tomorrow is a new day!
        A B C   D

5. Speak about your dream is the first step in making your dream come true.
     A   B   C   D

单元检测

第一部分 英语知识运用(共分三节,满分40分)

第一节 语音知识:从 A、B、C、D 四个选项中找出画线部分与所给单词画线部分读音相同的选项。(共5分,每小题1分)

(　　)1. photography　　A. employ　　B. satisfy　　C. yesterday　　D. sky

(　　)2. honor　　A. hockey　　B. holiday　　C. hole　　D. honest

(　　)3. chop　　A. Christmas　　B. stomach　　C. Chinese　　D. chemistry

(　　)4. digestion　　A. recognition　　B. question　　C. education　　D. graduation

( )5. voyage   A. German   B. goal   C. garden   D. weight

第二节　词汇与语法知识：从 A、B、C、D 四个选项中选出可以填入空白处的最佳选项。（共 25 分，每小题 1 分）

( )6. During the internship, the boss was satisfied _____ my communication skills.
A. on   B. in   C. by   D. with

( )7. We spent our summer vacation _____ the elderly as volunteers in the community.
A. help   B. to help   C. helping   D. helped

( )8. This is the place where children can practice _____.
A. to sing   B. singing   C. sing   D. sang

( )9. Diana was praised for her _____ performance in the speech competition.
A. outstand   B. outstanding   C. outstood   D. standing

( )10. I can catch my flight _____ I arrive at the airport before 11 a. m.
A. as soon as   B. as far as   C. as long as   D. as well as

( )11. What's more, taking _____ food photos is a must.
A. to amazing   B. amaze   C. amazing   D. amazed

( )12. They insisted that he _____ a job and work on a regular basis.
A. find   B. found   C. finds   D. finding

( )13. _____ business online is now a fashion.
A. To do   B. Doing   C. Done   D. Does

( )14. He was keen _____ repairing cars and good at it.
A. in   B. on   C. with   D. out

( )15. Wu Wei was a careful and _____ person.
A. respond   B. response   C. responsibly   D. responsible

( )16. Take some spare clothes _____ you get wet.
A. in case   B. in case of   C. including   D. include

( )17. The matter _____ your fate cannot be taken for granted.
A. relating to   B. related to   C. relate to   D. to relate to

( )18. I believe the audiences will be deeply _____ the story.
A. impress by   B. impressed by   C. interested in   D. prefer to

( )19. A makerspace is a place _____ innovators gather to share resources and knowledge to make their dreams come true.
A. which   B. that   C. where   D. on which

( )20. He used to _____ in a small village, but now he has been used to _____ in the big city.
A. live; living   B. live; live   C. living; living   D. living; live

(   )21. Then enjoy _____ your dream come true.
    A. making   B. make   C. made   D. to make

(   )22. We didn't want him to look foolish and _____.
    A. laughed at   B. laughing at   C. laugh at   D. be laughed at

(   )23. Though I've always wanted to be a novelist, _____ I'm afraid of telling others.
    A. but   B. /   C. or   D. and

(   )24. He is _____ his great success in scientific researches.
    A. pride of   B. pride in   C. proud of   D. proud in

(   )25. You should be more _____ to realise your dream.
    A. confidents   B. confidence   C. confidently   D. confident

(   )26. _____ we do, we should make an effort.
    A. Whenever   B. Whatever   C. However   D. Wherever

(   )27. The important thing is to know what you want, and then do everything you can _____ your dream.
    A. to realise   B. realise   C. impress   D. to impress

(   )28. Oversleeping will never make your dreams _____.
    A. come ture   B. come with   C. come up   D. come out

(   )29. He is often made _____ for twelve hours a day by his boss.
    A. work   B. working   C. to work   D. to be working

(   )30. I want the work _____ properly. I'm the only one who can do it right.
    A. do   B. be done   C. to be done   D. to do

第三节 完形填空：阅读下面的短文，从所给的 A、B、C、D 四个选项中选出正确的答案。(共 10 分，每小题 1 分)

Every school has rules for students to follow. However, some students may see the __31__ as a way which teachers control them. Sometimes, they're unhappy and even feel __32__. Well, if you think your life is hard, you might think about the __33__ in ancient times. For some of them, life was really hard.

In the old days, people believed that teachers had to be very __34__ and had the right to punish the students. Parents didn't mind if teachers punished their children when their children didn't do what they were __35__ to do. Often, the stricter a teacher was, the more parents thought he or she was a good teacher.

In fact, following school rules can be very important. For example, running in the hallways could cause a student to __36__. It may hurt himself or another person. Following the rules can also help the students in the classroom to learn __37__ difficulty. In class, a teacher may ask students to raise their hands __38__ they speak. If someone speaks out of turn, other students might not be able to hear the teacher __39__. School rules can help students prepare for their own futures as well. When they 40 and go out on their own, they'll soon find that they still need to follow rules.

Rules make the world much better. If there are no rules, life will be meaningless and in disorder.

( )31. A. rules   B. excuses   C. facts   D. examples
( )32. A. tired   B. angry   C. excited   D. good
( )33. A. doctors   B. parents   C. teachers   D. students
( )34. A. kind   B. clever   C. strict   D. careful
( )35. A. told   B. heard   C. invited   D. watched
( )36. A. come out   B. fall down   C move on   D pass by
( )37. A. about   B. from   C. except   D. without
( )38. A. because   B. though   C. before   D. unless
( )39. A. clearly   B. luckily   C. quickly   D. politely
( )40. A. hurry up   B. look up   C. grow up   D. dress up

第二部分　篇章与词汇理解(共分三节,满分50分)

第一节　阅读理解,阅读下列短文,从每题所给的A、B、C、D四个选项中,选出最恰当的答案。(共30分,每小题2分)

A

You must have dreams and goals in your life. To succeed, you need to make your dream become a burning desire. If you look at the successful people in the world, you'll find the only thing they have in common is that they want something and they go to get it. These people have different education and backgrounds. But they all have a burning desire to succeed.

When I was new in sales, I had become one of the top salesmen in my company. I worked hard every day and dreamed about becoming a manager. After 18 months, I applied for the position but got the answer, "You are a valuable salesman, sorry." I was very disappointed. At last, I realized that it was up to me if I was going to be a manager. I started working hard again, harder than ever before. Within 5 months, I became a manager successfully. The only reason why I got the position was that I wanted it very much.

Anything you dream about can be yours if you want it. Sooner or later your dream will come true and you will have what you have wanted.

( )41. What does the underlined word "desire" probably mean?
　　　 A. 欲望   B. 火焰   C. 火柴   D. 蜡烛
( )42. The writer wants to be a _____.
　　　 A. salesman   B. manager   C. rich man   D. teacher
( )43. How long did it take the writer to make his dream come true?

A. 5 months　　B. 13 months　　C. 18 months　　D. 23 months

(　)44. What can we learn from the passage?

A. The successful people have the same background.

B. The successful people have some strange ideas.

C. The writer is good at selling things to others.

D. The writer doesn't like his job at all.

(　)45. The passage talks about how to _____.

A. realize the dream　　　　B. get good education

C. tell the truth　　　　　　D. set up a goal

B

Each of us has dreams and goals for our future. What makes us study and make progress each day is closely connected with our personal dream and goal.

But why do you have dreams and goals, you still end up with nothing? What separates successful people from the dreamers is their persistent (锲而不舍的) action. When you learn your lessons in school, you must work hard and not give up. You will often find some of your lessons very hard. Try and keep trying, and you'll be sure to successfully deal with any difficulty you meet with. If we have a hard lesson today, let us try our best to learn it well and then we shall be prepared for a harder one tomorrow.

This is the famous formula(公式) for success：

Dream > Believe > Achieve

Most people have what they want (Dream) and think they can realize their dreams (Believe). And then they do nothing. They just imagine their dreams can come true. When they get tired waiting and lose a lot, they get bored. They say angrily how terrible their life is.

I personally believe that if you really want to achieve your dreams and goals in life, you have to add one thing to your success formula：

Dream > Believe > Act > Achieve

For me, act is the most important thing for success and that's to Take Persistent Action (Act). If you say, "I can't do it" and give up, you can never do anything valuable. However, "I'll try" creates wonders. Let's remember that there will be obstacles in our life. We must face them bravely and solve them. Success is not something that falls down from the sky. Most successful people made their dreams come true because of their persistent action.

Please remember：Action is the bridge that connects our dreams and goals to reality.

(　)46. What should you do when you find your lessons very hard?

A. Ask people for help.　　　　B. Try and keep trying.

C. Get ready to create wonders.　D. Prepare for a harder one.

(　)47. Which does the writer add to the famous formula?

A. Act.　　　　B. Achieve.　　C. Connect.　　D. Create.

(　)48. What does the underlined word "obstacles" mean?

A. Dangers.　　B. Imaginations.　C. Wonders.　　D. Difficulties.

(　)49. Why does the writer use the formula "Dream > Believe > Act > Achieve"?

A. To support his idea.　　　　B. To ask readers to explain it.

C. To show what his goals are.　D. To compare it with a bridge.

(　)50. Which of the following can be the best title for the passage?

A. Doing Something Valuable

B Studying Hard and Making Progress

C. Realizing Dreams with Persistent Action

D. Separating Successful People from Dreamers

C

Brian was a funny student. He loved watching comedies(喜剧) best and hoped to become a comedy actor one day.

When he heard about the talent show to be held at his school, Brian decided to take part in. He had never acted on stage before, and he was very excited. But some students laughed at him. "You are not funny but silly," Ken, one of his classmates, said to his face. "No one will l ike what you do." another boy also said to him, loudly.

Brian couldn't understand why they were so unkind to him. For a moment, he thought about giving up the show. But he remembered how much his friends liked his jokes, and also his teachers said he was very funny. So he decided to prepare for the show.

Brian did a great job at the talent show. Everyone loved his performance, and he won the first prize! His teachers and friends were proud of him. Even so, Ken told Brian that he was not funny, and that he would never be successful. Brian didn't understand why Ken said so, but he realized that it had nothing to do with him. He confidently continued to work towards his goal.

As the years went on, Brian met more people like Ken. "You'll do a terrible job," they said to him. Luckily, most people encouraged him and some helped him to become even funnier. He got a lot of opportunities to perform in movies. He was even invited to appear on television. His fans thanked him because his comedies made them feel good when they were unhappy.

Now Brian is a big comedy star! He is doing what he loves best. He never feels stressed like those unkind people, and he laughs all day long!

(　)51. What did Brian love best when he was a student?

A. Going to school.　　　B. Helping classmates.

C. Watching comedies.　　D. Meeting new friends.

(　)52. Brian decided to prepare for the show because _____.

A. his friends liked his jokes　　B. he was invited by a TV station

　　　　　　C. he wasn't busy acting in movies　　D. Ken was expecting his performance

(　　)53. After winning the first prize, Brian _____.
　　　　　A. began to understand Ken　　　　B. became a teacher of acting
　　　　　C. encouraged others to join him　　　D. continued to work towards his goal

(　　)54. Brian's fans thanked him because his comedies brought them _____.
　　　　　A. success　　　B. happiness　　　C. luck　　　D. pride

(　　)55. Which of the following can be the title of the passage?
　　　　　A. From Nobody to Somebody　　　B. People Like Ken
　　　　　C. A Funny Student　　　　　　　D. The Talent Show

第二节　词义搭配：从(B)栏中选出(A)栏单词的正确解释。(共10分，每小题1分)

　　　　　　(A)　　　　　　　　　　　　(B)

(　　)56. photography　　　A. public praise and reward for sb.'s work or actions
(　　)57. recommend　　　　B. the act of taking and printing photos
(　　)58. recognition　　　 C. a type of music with strong rhythms
(　　)59. envy　　　　　　D. the feeling of wanting sth. that sb. else has
(　　)60. outstanding　　　E. shy and nervous; not brave
(　　)61. timid　　　　　　F. people who have gathered to watch or listen to sth
(　　)62. sailor　　　　　　G. make attractive or acceptable; introduce
(　　)63. jazz　　　　　　 H. a person who works on a ship
(　　)64. audience　　　　 I. feeling or showing thanks
(　　)65. grateful　　　　　J. extremely good; excellent

第三节　补全对话，根据对话内容，从对话后的选项中选出能填入空白处的最佳选项。(共10分，每小题2分)

A: Hi, Jack. Last week our school held a an activity about dreams, did you attend?

B:　66　, because when I joined an activity last time, the activity was held so badly that I don't want to join any activities.

A: That's a shame. The activity was well organized. A lot of people delivered their dreams, and they all delivered very well. It made me feel great.

B: That's really a pity.

A:　67　

B: Go ahead.

A: What's your dream? And　68　

B: En… My dream is traveling around the world to enjoy different food and experience different cultures. When I was a child, I read a travel diary. The contents are very attractive to me. So I have a dream to travel around the world.

A:　69　. How do you achieve your dream?

B：I'll work hard and I'll quit my job to travel when I save enough money. I'll take my girlfriend with me if the conditions permit.

A：Wow, __70__.

B：Thank you.

> A. why do you have such a dream?
> B. Your dream sounds good.
> C. Can I ask you a few questions?
> D. I wish you can achieve your dream early.
> E. No, I don't like to join any activities.

第三部分　语言技能运用(共分四节,满分 30 分)

第一节　单词拼写：根据下列句子及所给汉语注释,在横线上写出单词的正确形式。(共 5 分,每小题 1 分)

71. Can you _____（推荐）a good hotel?

72. She still lived at home after _____（毕业）.

73. The men were _____（抓住）as they left the building.

74. He was forced to leave his _____（祖国）for political reasons.

75. The _____（观众）threw flowers onto the stage.

第二节　词形变换：用括号内单词的适当形式填空,将正确答案写在横线上。(共 5 分,每小题 1 分)

76. "Are you free tonight?" she asked _____（hopeful）.

77. Hellen got an A+ for her _____（outstand）essay and was praised by her teacher.

78. As a _____（musical）, she has spent years perfecting her technique.

79. Cao Xueqin, a great _____（novel）in the Qin Dynasty, wrote *Dream of Red Mansions*.

80. I _____（grateful）took the cup of coffee she offered me.

第三节　改错：从 A、B、C、D 四个画线处找出一处有错误的选项,并写出正确答案。(共 10 分,每小题 2 分)

81. I <u>could</u> travel <u>around</u> the world <u>recommend</u> delicious food <u>to</u> people.
　　　A　　　　　B　　　　　　　C　　　　　　　D

82. The boss was <u>satisfied</u> <u>by</u> my <u>communication</u> <u>skills</u>.
　　　　　　　　　A　　　　B　　　　C　　　　　　D

83. I was <u>amazing</u> and <u>deeply</u> <u>impressed</u> <u>by</u> Wu Wei and his story.
　　　　　A　　　　　　B　　　　　C　　　　D

84. He asked <u>to</u> <u>send</u> <u>to</u> work <u>in</u> the countryside.
　　　　　　A　　B　　C　　　　　D

85. We have been reading books for ten minutes. Let's stop having a rest.
         A   B   C   D

81.(　　)应为_____　82.(　　)应为_____　83.(　　)应为_____

84.(　　)应为_____　85.(　　)应为_____

第四节　书面表达。(共 10 分)

假如你是李华,你的美国朋友 Tim 给你发来电子邮件,询问你有何梦想。请你给他回复电子邮件。

要求:

1. 字数:80~100 字

2. 主要内容包括:(1)你的梦想是什么?

　　　　　　　　(2)你为这个梦想做过什么?

　　　　　　　　(3)为实现梦想你还需要怎样努力?

_____
_____
_____
_____
_____
_____

参 考 答 案

Unit 1　A Small Change Can Solve the Problems of Many

Warming up

二、1. creative　2. dustbin　3. data cable　4. curious　5 solve

6. opinion　7. design　8. organize　9. broaden　10. application form

Listening and Speaking

一、1-5 BDBDA

二、1-5 CADEB

三、1-5 BACED

Reading and Writing

一、1. creative　2. permission　3. influenced　4. continuous　5. invent

6. dustbin　7. solve　8. activities　9. broaden　10. profession

二、1-5 CBACA　6-10 CABAC

三、1-5 ACDCD

四、情景模拟

A：Would you like to join our club?

B：I would like to, but can you tell me when your club was set up?

A：It was set up ten years ago, there are so many activities in our club, for example, travelling, taking photos and so on.

B: Sounds interesting, but how can I join your club?

A: Very easy, you just need to fill out an application form, then wait for telephone.

B: Thanks, I want to broaden my mind, and have a chance to practice what I have learned at school.

Grammar

一、1-5 BACCA 6-10 BCACB 11-15 DBCBC 16-20 CCBAC 21-25 CBCBD

26-30 BDACC

二、1. A 改为 whether 2. A 改为 whether 3. B 改为 whether 4. B 改为 turns

5. D 改为 the supermarket is 6. C 改为 I had 7. C 改为 had given

8. C if 改为 whether 9. B 改为 how 10. C 改为 who you are

More Activities

一、1-5 BAABC

二、1. be of increasing value 2. come up with 3. not only... but also...

4. by accident 5. such as 6. that's not the case

7. make one's mark 8. be exposed to 9. by nature 10. make up

三、1. Creativity 2. making 3. influenced 4. continued 5. invention

6. invented 7. Traditional 8. permitting 9. professional 10. activities

四、1. D 改为 to switch 2. C 改为 be operated 3. B 改为 hidden

4. A 改为 Thanks to 5. C 改为 invented

单元检测

第一部分

第一节 1-5 BBCBD

第二节 6-10 BABCA 11-15 BCBAC 16-20 AAACB 21-25 ABCBC

26-30 BCADD

第三节 31-35 ADBCB 36-40 ADCBA

第二部分

第一节 41-45 ABDAC 46-50 BCCDA 51-55 DDDBB

第二节 56-60 CDAEB 61-65 GHFJI

第三节 66-70 CEBDA

第三部分

第一节 71. envelope 72. creative 73. surroundings 74. influenced 75. solve

第二节 76. professional 77. permission 78. continuous 79. invent 80. broaden

第三节 81. C 改为 greater 82. D 改为 late 83. C 改为 what

84. B 改为 how you inserted 85. B 改为 why

第四节 书面表达

Creativity is important not only to individuals but also to our nation.

Creativity helps with problem-solving. Creative people have open, active minds. They are always looking for new ways to solve problems, which motivate innovations and increases efficiency.

Give you some time to play or relax. Most of us have come up with a great new idea while taking a walk or a shower.

Creativity encourages questions. When you need to figure out a solution, ask yourself as many questions as possible. Just brainstorming, and you will find some good ideas.

Unit 2 It's Always Nice to Be Polite

Warming up

二、1. upright 2. business card 3. punctual 4. open-minded 5. internship
6. make-up 7. etiquette 8. smoothly 9. awkward 10. improper

Listening and Speaking

一、1-5 ADADB

二、1-5 BACED

三、1-5 BADEC

四、情景模拟

My advice on internship etiquette

Internship etiquette plays an important role in our daily life. But do you know internship etiquette, if you want to do better in internship etiquette, you should make an effort during the internship, things will work out. I think you need to pay attention to different rules of etiquette. You should know dress code and punctuality. Dress smartly to make a good impression. Avoid wearing heavy make-up and strong perfume.

I'll keep your advice in mind.

Reading and Writing

一、1. stepping 2. exhausted 3. reminder 4. breath 5. designer
　　6. internship 7. gesture 8. punctual 9. Congratulations 10. employee

二、1-5 CBDBD 6-10 CBCDD

三、1-5 CBCAC

Grammar

一、1-5 BDDBD 6-10 ACBDB 11-15 BAACB 16-20 AADDD 21-25 BCDAA
　　26-30 BBCBD

二、1. A 改为 However 2. C 改为 when 3. C 改为 so 4. A 改为 Whether
　　5. D 改为 comes 6. C 改为 before 7. A 改为 Even though
　　8. B 改为 where 9. C 改为 if 10. A 改为 such

More Activities

一、1-5 CADBB

二、1. workplace behaviour 2. step into an office 3. on the board 4. be sure about
　　5. go to a quiet corner 6. make a call 7. put... back onto the shelf
　　8. turn off 9. take a deep breath 10. design some reminders

三、1. behaviour 2. emergency 3. smoothly 4. importance 5. embarrassing
　　6. colleagues 7. informal 8. mastered 9. reminders 10. respond

四、1. A 改为 If 2. A 改为 Before 3. A 改为 so 4. C 改为 when 5. B 改为 stick

单元检测

第一部分

第一节　1-5 ADCDA

第二节　6-10 CADAC　11-15 BABAA　16-20 BCAAA　21-25 BCABA

26-30 ACBAA

第三节　31-35 BDACB　36-40 AABAB

第二部分

第一节　41-45 DCADC　46-50 CADCB　51-55 DDADC

第二节　56-60 CABED　61-65 HFIGJ

第三节　66-70. CBADE

第三部分

第一节　71. internship　72. impression　73. behaviour　74. recognise　75. master

第二节　76. punctuality　77. properly　78. behave　79. summary　80. frighten

第三节　81. A 改为 brief　82. D 改为 disturbed　83. C 改为 reminders

84. D 改为 widely　85. A 改为 Unless

第四节　书面表达

Workplace Etiquette Tips

Workplace etiquette is increasingly important and influences people's career success. Here are some useful etiquette tips for those who just start out in their career.

1. Fit in the corporate culture as soon as possible. Bear in mind and follow company's rules. Avoid going to work late or leaving work early. Don't make personal calls during work hours.

2. Start from basics. Get ready to do chores in the office, such as loading paper into the photocopier and loading the water dispenser with full water bottles. They make a good impression.

3. Be open-minded and consult with your colleagues. Asking questions is an effective way to solve problems, increase communication, and develop friendship.

Unit 3　We Are Part of Nature

Warming up

二、1. local produce　2. rubbish　3. public transport　4. packaging　5. recyclable

6. consumption　7. policy　8. efficient　9. tableware　10. discount

Listening and Speaking

一、1-5 ADDBA

二、1-5 CEDBA

三、1-5 CABED

四、情景模拟

A：Excuse me. Do you know the zero carbon day?

B：Yes, it is a day to call on us to save energy, it is the policy of our country.

A：With the development of our society, energy consumption is becoming larger and larger.

B：It is badly damage our environment.

A：So you need to know how to protect our environment.

B：Can you tell me some efficient ways to protect our environment? And how to celebrate the zero carbon day?

A：Yes, you should be equipped your mind with knowledge about environment and take actions to protect the environment.

Reading and Writing

一、1. environmental   2. global   3. discounted   4. optional   5. unwilling

6. flyer   7. supporting   8. efficient   9. healthy   10. Discounted

二、1-5 DBABD   6-10 DCABC

三、1-5 DCADB

四、书面表达

My opinion on environmental protection

As we all know, protecting the environment is very important. The earth is important to our lives. Water, air and plants are essential to the lives of humans and other animals. With the development of our society, we live more and more happily, but the problem of pollution is more and more serious.

In order to protect the environment, I have formed some good habits. First, I turn the tap off when I am not using it. In this way I can save water. Second, I use public transportation whenever possible to keep air clean. Third, I write on both sides of paper so that fewer trees are cut to be made into paper.

I hope some day we can see the blue sky and breathe fresh air again.

Grammar

一、1-5 DAABC　6-10 CCCDC　11-15 DDBCD　16-20 ABCDD　21-25 ADCDD

　　26-30 BDDCA

二、1. B 改为 watching　2. C 改为 killing　3. A 改为 Not knowing

　　4. B 改为 speaking　5. C 改为 drowning　6. D 改为 allowing

　　7. C 改为 lecturing　8. C 改为 preparing　9. D 改为 shopping

　　10. C 改为 singing

More Activities

一、1-5 ACCBC

二、1. "go green" activity　2. discounted vegetables and fruit　3. food court

　　4. bottled water　5. tap water　6. clothing exchange　7. global warming

　　8. outdoor activities　9. take part in　10. design a flyer

三、1. awareness　2. global　3. grasslands　4. survived　5. Handkerchiefs

　　6. activities　7. seasonal　8. protection　9. consumption　10. natural

四、1. C 改为 regretting　2. D 改为 healthy　3. B 改为 described　4. B 改为 willing

　　5. B 改为 clothing

单元检测

第一部分　英语知识运用

第一节　1-5 ABADC

第二节　6-10 DABAB　11-15 CACDA　16-20 CABAC　21-25 BCBBC

　　　　26-30 BCABA

第三节　31-35 BACDB　36-40 DACBD

第二部分　篇章与词汇理解

第一节　41-45. ABCBA　46-50 ACADD　51-55 ADCDB

第二节　56-60 CABED　61-65 GFJHI

第三节　66-70 CADBE

第三部分 语言技能应用

第一节 71. consumption 72. effective/efficient 73. discount 74. develop 75. processes

第二节 76. willing 77. survival 78. environmental 79. replace 80. emission

第三节 81. C 改为 with 82. C 改为 green 83. A 改为 living 84. D 改为 variety 85. C 改为 on

第四节 书面表达

It is our duty to protect environment. After learning about environment protection in school, I have learned to make a change in my life.

In the past, I went to school in my parents' car and I threw away all the things that were broken. Besides, I would ask for plastic bags when I was shopping. Now, I have realized the importance of protecting our environment. I go to school on foot or by bike. I use all my daily necessities as long as possible. Moreover, I get used to taking my own bag when shopping.

I think we students should be always aware of the importance of protecting the environment. We should save every drop of water and turn off lights when leaving the classroom.

Unit 4　Beauty Is About How You Feel

Warming up

二、1. 美,美感 2. delighted 3. 震惊的 4. handicraft 5. 和平的
6. design 7. 舒适的 8. beauty of sports 9. 有希望的 10. relaxed

Listening and Speaking

一、1-5 DACCD

二、1-5 DEBAC

三、1-5 CEADB

四、场景模拟

A：Jane, please come here. Look at this painting.

B：How amazing it is! It looks like the works of Xu Beihong.

A：Really? Let me watch it carefully.

B：See? I am interested in traditional Chinese paintings, especially Xu Beihong's.

A：Although I don't have research on it, I still feel the beauty of it.

B：Exactly! The exhibition is more interesting than expected.

A：Yes, I totally agree!

B：If you have any interests in traditional Chinese culture, shall we go to the museum next time?

A：Of course!

Reading and Writing

一、1. Beauty 2. relaxation 3. invisible 4. appreciated 5. silence
   6. attentive 7. unite 8. thunderstorm 9. explore 10. physical

二、1-5 BACCD 6-10 ABDCB

三、1-5 DDADC

四、书面表达

Beauty

There are many kinds of beauty, including external beauty and internal beauty, concrete beauty and abstract beauty, natural beauty and artificial beauty, etc.

Looking for beautiful things can help us find the true meaning of life and make us become better.

These beautiful things may just be small things around us. It may be a seat offer on the bus. It may be a "thank you" after receiving help. It may be the innocent smile on children's faces. It may be the scenery you see when you arrive at the top of the mountain with your friends.

Only when seeing with your heart is beauty everywhere.

Grammar

一、1-5 ABCAD 6-10 BABBC 11-15 AACCA 16-20 CBCBB 21-25 AABCD
   26-30 AABBB

二、1. How, hard 2. How, shocked 3. What, complicated 4. How, beautiful, it is
   5. Don't smoke here 6. Check your homework before you hand it in

7. Don't play in the street. It is dangerous

8. If necessary, we will finish it ahead of time

9. Your name and address, please   10. Well done

More Activities

一、1-5 ABBCA

二、1. 使我高兴起来   2. heart and soul   3. 对我们有好处   4. driving force
5. 跟随某人的内心   6. natural scenery   7. 一道闪电   8. classical music
9. 冉冉升起的太阳   10. handmade furniture   11. 清澈的眼眸   12. calm down

三、1. fantastic   2. classical   3. complicated   4. artistic   5. painting
6. kindness   7. powerful   8. satisfaction   9. amazing   10. delighted

四、1. B 改为 simplest   2. C 改为 full   3. B 改为 thirsty   4. A 改为 mere
5. B 改为 lack

单元检测

第一部分　英语知识运用

第一节　1-5 DCBDD

第二节　6-10 BACBD   11-15 ADBBC   16-20 BCDDC   21-25 CDCDD
26-30 BBABC

第三节　31-35 DCCAB   36-40 ACCDB

第二部分　篇章与词汇理解

第一节　41-45 CBBAD   46-50 CDDAB   51-55 ADBCD

第二节　56-60 DIEGH   61-65 JCBFA

第三节　66-70 CEBDA

第三部分　语言技能应用

第一节　71. invisible   72. appreciate   73. handicrafts   74. furniture   75. explore

第二节　76. relaxation   77. physical   78. shocked   79. artistic   80. natural

第三节　81. C 改为 does   82. B 改为 beauty
83. A 改为 What an 或者 B 改为 an interesting
84. C 改为 shall   85. D 改为 waiting

第四节　书面表达

Life is Full of Beauty

Beauty is everywhere around us. In our life, we can find a lot of beauty. And there are many beautiful people and things around us.

When it comes to the most beautiful person in my heart, it must be Mr. Zhang. He is my English teacher. He is not only a tall and handsome man but also patient and kind. I was poor in English before. Therefore, to improve my grades, he always taught me patiently after school, and he never complained about it. With his help, I have made great progress in English. We also built a deep relationship with each other.

Even though Mr. Zhang is a common person, he does well in his job as a teacher. So he is the most beautiful person in my heart.

Unit 5　It's Necessary to Develop Soft Skills

Warming up

二、1. 挑战　2. self-confidence　3. 解决方法　4. communication skills

　　5. 时间管理　6. positive attitude　7. 解决问题的能力　8. cooperate with

　　9. 令人赞叹的　10. participate in

Listening and Speaking

一、1-5 BACDA

二、1-5 CEDAB

三、1-5 BDEAC

四、场景模拟

A: Hello, is that Mr. Brown?

B: Yes, it is. Who's calling, please?

A: I'm from the package delivery company. I have your package. Are you at home?

B: Unfortunately, I'm at work right now. Can you leave the package at my door?

A: Actually, this package needs your name. Can I bring it to your office instead?

B: I'm quite busy at work now. I don't have time to leave my desk.

A:I see. Well, can I bring the package tomorrow?

B:Yes, that would be better. Can you bring it to my home at 6 p.m.?

A:Sure, that is fine. I will see you tomorrow at 6 p.m.

B:Great, thank you so much!

Reading and Writing

一、1. technical   2. interpersonal   3. necessity   4. competition   5. co-workers
   6. compete   7. skills   8. persuade   9. faced   10. cooperate

二、1-5 ACDBB   6-10 AACBD

三、1-5 ABBDD

四、书面表达

Xin Hua Middle School

Wanted: English teacher

Skills required:

* solid knowledge about English language

* solid knowledge about English teaching

* basic computer skill

* strong communication skills

* interpersonal skills

* problem-solving skills

* creative thinking

* responsible and patient

Grammar

一、1-5 CCBBD   6-10 ABBBA   11-15 DDBBB   16-20 ACBBD
   21-25 DBCAD   26-30 DADDD

二、1. C 改为 working   2. A 改为 Not   3. C 改为 going out   4. D 改为 to happen
   5. D 改为 being seen   6. A 改为 Being   7. D 改为 being killed
   8. A 改为 Not having   9. D 改为 breaking   10. A 改为 Watching

More Activities

一、1-5 CABAD

二、1. 创新思维   2. team spirit   3. 人际交往能力   4. job performance
   5. 职场礼仪   6. career planning   7. 管理能力   8. problem-solving skill
   9. 积极的态度   10. communication skill

三、1. planning   2. positive   3. Interpersonal   4. spirit   5. communication
   6. performance   7. solved   8. management   9. creative   10. practical

四、1. D 改为 to describe   2. A 改为 demanding   3. B 改为 had
   4. C 改为 given   5. D 改为 with

单元检测

第一部分　英语知识运用

第一节　1-5 CDCBB

第二节　6-10 BABDD   11-15 DDACA   16-20 CDBDB   21-25 BBBBC
    26-30 ABCBC

第三节　31-35 CDDAB   36-40 CCBDA

第二部分　篇章与词汇理解

第一节　41-45 ADABC   46-50 DCACB   51-55 BCADC

第二节　56-60 BIAED   61-65 GFJCH

第三节　66-70 CDABE

第三部分　语言技能应用

第一节　71. cooperate   72. handle   73. technique   74. schedule   75. disappointed

第二节　76. impressive   77. solution   78. necessary   79. challenging   80. competition

第三节　81. D 改为 participate in   82. D 改为 to compete   83. D 改为 to build
    84. C 改为 crying   85. B 改为 finishing

第四节　书面表达

Soft Skills

Soft skills are necessary to us nowadays. They include interpersonal skills and self-management abilities, such as the ability to communicate, cooperate, organise the work and so on.

Different from hard skills, soft skills more reflect people's ability to solve problems creatively. For example, when my team members have different ideas on a problem, I usually talk with them, analyse the problem and choose the best way to solve it.

Of course, soft skills require our continuous learning and training. And I believe that as long as we insist, we will surely have them.

Unit 6　It's like a Home Away from Home

Warming up

二、1. 社区服务　2. raise money　3. 捐衣服　4. benefit　5. 组织　6. sign up

　　7. 成功　8. sense of belonging　9. 信赖，依靠　10. come across

　　11. 装饰，布置　12. out of trouble

Listening and Speaking

一、1-5　CABBC

二、1-5　CEABD

三、1-5　ECDBA

四、模拟对话

A: Hello! May I speak to Frank, please?

B: Speaking.

A: Hey, Frank! This is John. Do you have any idea about this weekend?

B: Yes, I'll take part in the "Tree Planting Day" activity in my community.

A: Wow! What will you do there?

B: We'll go to plant trees in the People's Park. It is about the green life style.

A: It's great and meaningful.

B: Yes. Do you want to go with me?

A: Of course!

B: OK. See you then!

Reading and Writing

一、1. decorating   2. to enter   3. exchanging   4. Serving   5. needed
   6. to pass   7. seek   8. importance   9. living   10. volunteering

二、1-5 BDCBC   6-10 ADACB

三、1-5 BCABD

四、书面表达

To Be a Community Volunteer

We are high school students and we are busy with our lessons. So some people think we should concentrate more on our studies. If we volunteer to help others, it's a waste of time. But I think volunteering is great.

I not only feel good about helping others, but also get to spend time doing what I love to do. And from volunteering I have learned many things that I have never learned in class. So if I have a chance, I'd like to visit old people's houses to clean up for them. I'd also like to help sick kids in hospital. I love kids and I plan to put my love to good use by working in a hospital.

In a word, I'd like to help people who need help. If everyone helps out a bit, the world will be more colorful.

Grammar

一、1-5 BCBAC   6-10 ABCCD   11-15 ADBDC   16-20 CABAB   21-25 ADACD
   26-30 CCACB

二、1. A 改为 Those   2. C 改为 that   3. A 改为 As   4. B 改为 when   5. B 去掉 it
   6. C 改为 are   7. D 改为 that   8. A 改为 without   9. D 改为 whom   10. C 改为 as

More Activities

一、1-5 BABCB

二、1. community service   2. 偶遇   3. pass on love   4. 爱护公共财产
   5. surf the Internet   6. 教学助理   7. be good/bad for   8. 和……一样重要
   9. seek advice   10. 参与,参加   11. design posters   12. 归属感

三、1. involved   2. to text   3. feel   4. Teaching   5. tiring   6. connections

7. strengthened　8. organisation　9. importance　10. healthy

四、1. C 改为 for　2. B 改为 needed　3. C 去掉 it　4. D 改为 were written

5. B 改为 against

单元检测

第一部分

第一节　1-5 CADCD

第二节　6-10 ACCBA　11-15 ABDBC　16-20 CABAD　21-25 ACBBD

26-30 CABCC

第三节　31-35 ABBCD　36-40 CCBAA

第二部分

第一节　41-45 BDABC　46-50 BDDBB　51-55 CCDDA

第二节　56-60 FJAHC　61-65 IBDEG

第三节　66-70 BEDCA

第三部分

第一节　71. convenient　72. strangers　73. gain　74. experience　75. connection

第二节　76. succeed　77. belief　78. individuals　79. relied　80. service

第三节　81. C 改为 I have seen　82. B 改为 easier　83. C 改为 to enter

84. D 改为 playing　85. B 去掉 it

第四节　写作

Learning from Lei Feng

　　Lei Feng is known as a pattern that offered help to others selflessly. He devoted all this life to his beloved career as well. I was totally shocked by his character. And more and more people begin to learn from him.

　　To help others is not a hard thing. However, what you need is to do what you can do to help others and insist on doing it. Take myself for example, I often take part in community service, go to the old people's homes to help them clean their rooms and sing songs for them. Besides, I donate my spare money to those students whose families are poor. And I often give my seats to the old and people with little babies.

　　I strongly propose that we shall see a better world if each of us treats Lei Feng as our model and copies his spirit.

Unit 7 High Technology Has Really Changed Our Life

Warming up

二、1. 高速列车   2. no longer   3. 共享单车   4. electric toothbrush   5. 新能源汽车

6. remind sb to do sth   7. 无人驾驶汽车   8. get hooked on   9. 游轮

10. floor mopping robot

Listening and Speaking

一、1-5 ACCBD

二、1-5 ECBDA

三、1-5 BCAED

四、模拟对话

A：What are you doing on the Internet?

B：I'm booking the ticket. I want to go home by train.

A：Online? I usually book it through the Mobile phone railway ticket reservation system. I think it is more convenient.

B：Yes. But I am currently using computer.

A：Now booking train tickets online is more convenient and rapicler compared with buying them over the counter at railway stations where one has to wait for a long time.

B：You are right. I waited for several hours before.

A：Later, people can purchase tickets by phone.

B：In short, technology makes our life easier.

Reading and Writing

一、1. treasures   2. negative   3. Therefore   4. firm   5. experiment

6. unpacked   7. interrupting   8. enjoy   9. pressed   10. deleted

二、1-5 ACCCD   6-10 ADADC

三、1-5 ABDAC

四、书面表达

Can Students Use Cell Phones?

Cell phones have become more and more popular in China recently. Wherever you go, you can see people using cell phones. Many high school students have cell phones.

Cell phones have brought people a lot of benefits, but the most important is that they are convenient. With cell phones in their hands, they can keep in touch with anybody they want. If they want to get some information from the internet, they can easily have their dream realized via cell phones too.

However, cell phones can also bring people problems. The most serious is the electric wave radiation which is thought to be harmful to users' brains. Another problem is that when people are having a meeting or having a class or at a concert etc, the ring of the cell phone may interrupt others. I think students should use cellphones as little as possible and turn them off when they are attending important meetings or classes.

Grammar

一、1-5 CCAAC 6-10 DCADA 11-15 DDDBB 16-20 CBBCA 21-25 CCDDC
26-30 BBADC

二、1. C 改为 was 2. B 改为 have 3. D 改为 has been dead 4. B 改为 did
5. B 改为 have been cut 6. C 改为 had 7. D 改为 is 8. C 改为 have been
9. D 改为 were 10. A 改为 arrived

More Activities

一、1-5 ACADA

二、1. far away from 2. 与……交流 3. remind… of 4. 对……有害 5. focus on
6. 花费……在…… 7. relay race 8. 电子书 9. in favour of 10. 由于

三、1. technology 2. inconvenient 3. communicating 4. harmful 5. favoured
6. effective 7. variety 8. hooked 9. favoured 10. broadcasting

四、1. C 改为 on 2. D 改为 while 3. B 改为 convenient 4. B 改为 no 5. A 去掉 was

单元检测

第一部分

第一节　1-5 CBBAC

第二节　6-10 BADAC　11-15 BBABC　16-20 BAACD　21-25 BBCAD
　　　　26-30 CABAB

第三节　31-35 BAACC　36-40 ACABB

第二部分

第一节　41-45 ACBBD　46-50 ADCDA　51-55 ADCDB

第二节　56-60 EDGJA　61-65 IHCFB

第三节　66-70 BECAD

第三部分

第一节　71. favor　72. experiment　73. spaceship　74. negative　75. Nowadays

第二节　76. obviously　77. interrupted　78. Distance　79. technology　80. reminded

第三节　81. A 改为 no　82. A 改为 not　83. A 改为 Owning　84. B 改为 been in
　　　　85. B 改为 harm

第四节　写作

Technology and Life

Technology has a great influence in my life and it also changes my life style. The technology that I want to talk about is the computer and telephone.

First, computer has the largest effect on my life. I do not need to sit in the library in order to get information. Also, I can sit at home and shop online which save much time for me. It is very convenient and helpful for me because I can stay home and know everything happens in the world. Secondly, telephone changes the way how people communicate with each other. People do not need to write letters to each other nowadays. Instead, we can just simply call up each other in order to communicate. It is much faster than writing letters.

In conclusion, technology has a great influence in the society as well as my life. My lifestyle has been changed due to the development of technology. Technology makes my life much easier!

Unit 8　I Have a Dream

Warming up

二、1. 减肥　2. practise doing　3. 乘坐热气球飞行　4. overcome my fear

　　5. 有一次机会　6. take action　7. 做更多锻炼　8. seize opportunities

　　9. 获取相关知识　10. study hard

Listening and Speaking

一、1-5 BADBB

二、1-5 EADCB

三、1-5 DBAEC

四、模拟对话

A：What did you dream of becoming when you were a little child?

A：I dreamt of becoming a painter. When I was a child, I loved painting a variety of things such as beautiful butterfly, vast sea, starry sky etc. The world is full of fascinating creatures. I want to show the world with my painting brush.

B：Wow, what a beautiful dream!

A：What about you?

B：I wanted to be a hairstylist when I was a child, because in my heart, the hands of the hairstylists are magical. They can make girls more beautiful and make boys more handsome only by a pair of scissors. I want to possess this magic.

A：It sounds pretty cool.

B：But as I grow up, I don't dream of being a hairstylist anymore, I want to be a teacher now, but it seems far from me.

A：Never give up, then you will get it.

B：Opportunities favor prepared mind.

A：Come on, girl!

Reading and Writing

一、1. mechanic 2. recognition 3. department 4. outstanding 5. novelist
　　6. impression 7. Employers 8. promoted 9. responsibilities 10. recognized

二、1-5 CDAAC   6-10 ABACD

三、1-5 ABBCA

四、书面表达

My Dream

Everybody has his dream. I also have my dream. My dream is to work for foreign tourists as a tour guide.

Why do I want to be a tour guide? First of all, I'm an outgoing girl and I like doing some exciting things. Maybe being a tour guide is the best choice. If I become a tour guide, I can travel all around China and know more about our country. Then I will tell the foreign tourists about our colorful history. Second, I like making friends. If I work as a tour guide, I can make a lot of friends all over the world. This may be great. Perhaps someday my foreign friends will ask me to visit their countries. I really like to go to their countries to know something about their culture. What's more, I like singing. Singing English songs is my favorite thing. I believe I will be popular with foreign tourists. Their trip will be excellent.

Now I am still a middle school student. My job now is to work hard at school. Then I'll go to university to learn something about being a tour guide. I'm sure I can be a qualified tour guide in the future.

Grammar

一、1-5 CDABA   6-10 BBBDA   11-15 ACACA   16-20 DDCAA   21-25 ACCDC
　　26-30 BBCAD

二、1. C 改为 to wait   2. C 改为 to speak   3. D 改为 In order not to   4. B 改为 to call
　　5. B 改为 to   6. C 改为 to finish   7. B 改为 not to   8. 去掉 C   9. C 改为 to enter
　　10. B 改为 to know

More Activities

一、1-5 DADAA

二、1. make a voyage in space   2. 精心照顾   3. open a clinic   4. 实现

5. learn an instrument   6. 与……讨论   7. be interested in   8. 梦想做某事

9. tour guide   10. 着陆、落到……上

三、1. organisation   2. audiences   3. interested   4. tourism   5. gratefully

6. satisfied   7. insisted   8. envied   9. Hopefully   10. pretending

四、1. C 改为 to see   2. C 改为 doesn't   3. B 改为 to do   4. C 改为 not

5. A 改为 Speaking

单元检测

第一部分

第一节   1-5 ADCBA

第二节   6-10 DCBBC   11-15 CABBD   16-20 ABBCA   21-25 ADBCD

26-30 BAACC

第三节   31-35 ABDCA   36-40 BDCAC

第二部分

第一节   41-45 ABDCA   46-50 BADAC   51-55 CADBA

第二节   56-60 BGADJ   61-65 EHCFI

第三节   66-70 ECABD

第三部分

第一节   71. recommend   72. graduation   73. seized   74. homeland   75. audience

第二节   76. hopefully   77. outstanding   78. musician   79. novelist   80. gratefully

第三节   81. C 改为 recommending   82. B 改为 with   83. A 改为 amazed

84. B 改为 be sent   85. D 改为 to have

第四节   写作

Dear Tim,

How's it going? As we all know, it's important for us to have dreams. My dream is to be a doctor because a doctor can cure people and even save people's lives.

I still remembered what happened when I was a middle school student. I often went to the local hospital to see what doctors were doing on weekends. Sometimes I even played games about being doctors and patients. Not only was it interesting but also was educative. However, I will try my best to be admitted by my ideal medical university. In that case, it will be easier for me to be a doctor. Only in this way can I realize my dream more easily. What's your dream? Look forward to hearing from you.

 Yours,
 Li Hua